MW00352884

My Presidential Life

My Presidential Life

*The Showdown at Putin's Dacha and Other Misadventures
on the Diplomatic Road*

Judd Swift

LYONS
PRESS

Essex, Connecticut

An imprint of Globe Pequot, the trade division of
The Rowman & Littlefield Publishing Group, Inc.
4501 Forbes Blvd., Ste. 200
Lanham, MD 20706
www.rowman.com

Distributed by NATIONAL BOOK NETWORK

Copyright © 2024 by Judd Swift

All rights reserved. No part of this book may be reproduced in any form or by any electronic or
mechanical means, including information storage and retrieval systems, without written permission
from the publisher, except by a reviewer who may quote passages in a review.

British Library Cataloguing in Publication Information available

Library of Congress Cataloging-in-Publication Data

Names: Swift, Judd, author.
Title: My presidential life: the showdown at Putin's dacha and other misadventures on the
    diplomatic road / Judd Swift.
Other titles: Showdown at Putin's dacha and other misadventures on the diplomatic road
Description: Essex, Connecticut: Lyons Press, [2024] | Includes index.
Identifiers: LCCN 2023040442 (print) | LCCN 2023040443 (ebook) | ISBN 9781493081486
    (hardcover) | ISBN 9781493081493 (epub)
Subjects: LCSH: Swift, Judd. | Presidents—United States—Staff—Biography. | United
    States—Politics and government—1989—Anecdotes. | United States—Politics and
    government—1981–1989—Anecdotes. | Presidents—United States—Biography—Anecdotes. |
    United States. Department of Energy—Officials and employees—Biography.
Classification: LCC E840.8.S94 A3 2024 (print) | LCC E840.8.S94 (ebook) | DDC 973.927092
    [B]—dc23/eng/20231031
LC record available at https://lccn.loc.gov/2023040442
LC ebook record available at https://lccn.loc.gov/2023040443

∞™ The paper used in this publication meets the minimum requirements of American National
Standard for Information Sciences—Permanence of Paper for Printed Library Materials, ANSI/
NISO Z39.48-1992.

Contents

Contents

Introduction

The acid test for any lifetime endeavor, I guess, would be to ask oneself, "Would I do it again?" Would I put up with the tension, the long and often sleepless nights, the thousands of hours on cramped airplanes flying around the globe when I hated flying?

Yes, I would. I would happily do it all again in a heartbeat—including the flying.

I began training for the job long before I knew such a job existed. In fact, I was learning the necessary skills long before I would serendipitously find myself involved in presidential advance work—and that it would become an occupation I'd love and pursue enthusiastically for close to twenty years.

Being a manager of American presidential appearances on the national and world stage was not the sort of job one heard about or saw in the want ads: PRESIDENTIAL ADVANCE MAN NEEDED: PREVIOUS EXPERIENCE HELPFUL.

Working in presidential advance required from every member of our talented team a knowledge of diplomacy and foreign affairs, a layered and nuanced sense of history, the wisdom of an experienced psychoanalyst, the patience of Job, and the finely tuned sense of a psychic.

We would plan presidential trips well ahead of time. A team member or two would always travel to the site a week or two beforehand to get the lay of the land and a sense of how the local population anticipated welcoming the president of the United States, not always with open arms.

We would plan motorcade routes, security, banquet seating arrangements, and media interviews. We'd work with the press to find the best angles for newsreels and photos. We'd plan accommodations and access for the always large group of aides and hangers-on who inevitably traveled with the president. We'd work with the Secret Service to assure the most important part of any trip, the president's life.

Every single trip was painstakingly choreographed.

The world's eyes are on an American president when he appears at a summit meeting overseas or makes a major domestic speech. My job was to ensure those eyes were sympathetic and admiring. Every move a president makes takes on symbolic power. I would work with my team behind the scene, setting the stage for those remarks.

Nine times out of ten, things would work out, or at least come close. But there was always the danger of a major catastrophe lingering nearby, ready to pounce.

That is what made my time in advance work for Ronald Reagan, George H. W. Bush, and George W. Bush the most interesting job I've ever had.

My preparation for my advance career began at my family's dining room table. I would listen and learn from the discussions of the sort of wide-ranging topics that arise when one's family happens to own the *Washington Evening Star*, a leading newspaper in Washington, DC—at a time when newspapers held great sway and were followed religiously by readers of all political stripes—and I was no stranger to hearing the inside stories of what was going on behind the scenes. This would prove invaluable later when I was in a foreign country ahead of a summit.

The *Star*, my family's paper, was the leading favorite among conservatives, and I inherited my family's leanings.

My advance career led me through the administrations of three champion conservatives. I was among the few administrative officials trusted to make sure their ventures into world and national affairs went off flawlessly. While such work might sound sublime, juggling myriad details, oversized egos, and high-pressure schedules timed to the second, the work was something akin to herding cats—a white-knuckle affair in which nothing was certain but uncertainty.

I relished the opportunity and came to think of myself as a field hand—an essential cog whose work in the shadows of history helped present to the world the great messages many look to from American presidents.

The symbolic, sweeping, and emotional message George H. W. Bush brought to Poland as Lech Wałęsa's Solidarity Party rose to power against the rusty Eastern Bloc leaders of the country come to mind. And, as it does, I also think of my own encounter with Wałęsa, who was a bit of a bully.

My meetings with Wałęsa, and with others, were proof that in advance work, anything could happen, and surprises were rarely pleasant. Take the time George H. W. Bush's motorcade took a wrong turn in Detroit, or when Vladimir Putin essentially kidnapped George W. Bush, or when a blustering Ted Kennedy tried to insert himself into an event Nancy and Ronald Reagan had not invited him to.

Advance work provided hard answers to questions I did not know enough to ask. I would learn, believe me. Take American unions—a robust and vital voting bloc whose support was long sought by both Democrats and Republicans.

My unspoken question at the time was: Are unions that important?

The answer was an unequivocal "yes."

Ronald Reagan changed that in 1980, when a new demographic, the Reagan Democrat, arose and helped propel him to the White House. Teamsters Union president Jackie Presser made sure his group would support Reagan again in 1984, and I was assigned the task of making sure Presser and his colleagues were happy. There were moments during my effort to arrange a Teamsters greeting for Vice President George H. W. Bush in New Jersey that gave me pause, though, that had me thinking, however briefly, that I might not live through the evening.

It all worked out.

I learned the other side of the union coin—again a reminder of the importance of the American labor movement—when, less than a week later, George H. W. Bush was nearly overwhelmed by an angry mob of steelworkers in Pennsylvania.

With the wrong sort of luck, at best, such incidents could dissolve into embarrassing and much publicized media coverage; at worst, such incidents could prove disastrous. I considered myself lucky because none of those incidents blew up and were essentially passed over by reporters. But I made my own luck by thorough and painstaking preparation for every trip I was involved in.

These were the types of foul-ups that made an advance man's nights sleepless and his career very short if they didn't end well.

I managed to keep the job over the years, so I must have done something right. That was another thing about being a presidential advance man. I knew things went well when I returned to Washington and heard nothing more after a trip. My main task was to set things up, then disappear; advance people are never meant to be seen and certainly never praised. But believe me, when something goes wrong, we are the first to be put under the klieg lights and blamed.

I had known nothing about advance work until the run-up to the 1980 presidential election, when I volunteered to help George H. W. Bush during his Republican primary race against Ronald Reagan.

At the time I was happy with my job in the hotel industry. Little did I know my connections and knowledge would thrust me into some of the most memorable events of my life, with world leaders, international drama, and an occasional close call with total disaster.

I came upon my advance career by chance—an unexpected and surprising turn of events. But, as I mentioned, I could not have been more prepared for it.

I got from my family a respect for conservative politics, which drew me to George H. W. Bush, the beginning of my long journey through presidential politics and the many summit meeting trips I supervised.

I got from my uncle, Smith Hempstone, a frequent dinner visitor at our house and a leading conservative columnist and later ambassador, an appreciation for how the media views a presidential event. Knowing what reporters were looking for, and the hard work they put in to get a story, helped me immensely in advance work.

When my father's concert career led us around Europe while it was recovering from the devastation of World War II, I developed an appreciation for the value of diplomacy and the power of the United States. When we moved to The Hague, in the Netherlands, my mother, who was a friend of Secretary of State George C. Marshall, worked in an office for the Marshall Plan, which would provide $15 billion to help finance rebuilding efforts on the Continent. That was diplomacy as its best and most effective.

I would later develop strong survival instincts and a defiantly proud Americanism at an elite British boarding school, where I was the subject of much bullying. Being the only American at that school gave me a sense of strength and how to respond to bullies, something I used frequently in my endeavors on advance trips, none more so than dealing with the cantankerous Lech Wałęsa in Poland.

My English schoolboy days were a period in which I learned how to thrive as an outsider and as someone who grew to appreciate that other countries and other cultures do things differently from Americans—and that respect and appreciation served me well over my years in advance work, where I frequently dealt with foreign counterparts.

I suppose my graduate-level coursework in advance studies grew out of my time in the military, where I served as an MP in Germany. In the army I learned the necessity of understanding hierarchy and one's place in the order of things—essential in advance work, where we were never—ever—to stand out or be heard. My MP work also provided guidance on knowing when the time for diplomacy is over and the time for forceful negotiation has begun.

I knew where the lines were, and I knew when it was time to cross them to get things done in the interest of a president.

My career in the hotel industry helped me fine-tune my rapport with self-involved guests whose egos were unbound. It proved priceless to me when dealing with the elite politicos of both parties I encountered in advance work.

Looking back on it all, I can say I had a résumé made in heaven for an advance man.

Over those years, I would despair at the failure of governments and diplomacy on a trip to Auschwitz. I'd ride the streets of

Shanghai in a motorcycle sidecar, and I'd shake my head at how many times our meetings were wiretapped. I would learn to give a begrudging respect to my Russian counterparts, men I'd work with cautiously but frequently.

Breath-holding moments were as predictable as the rising sun. We'd dodge the notorious Shining Path guerrillas in Peru, butt heads with an imperious defender of Generalissimo Francisco Franco in Spain, and appall a French diplomat with our bull-in-a-china-shop arrival at a summit.

But we'd always pull it off, a feat that would appear to be transcendentally magical until one considered how much work we invested to make sure a trip went as best it could.

Looking back at it now, the rich and textured and truly wonderful experiences I had during my advance days proved extraordinarily productive for a job I hadn't known existed.

CHAPTER I

Auschwitz-Birkenau

THE AGREEMENT WHEN I SIGNED UP FOR THE JOB WAS TACIT—
unspoken but clearly understood. Advance staff were meant to
perform their duties and stay out of the way. We were to never get
involved in the debate. We were process, not diplomacy; we were
expected to add neither emotion nor opinion.

By the time I found myself in Krakow, Poland, in 2005 for
a solemn ceremony to commemorate the sixtieth anniversary of
the liberation of the infamous Auschwitz-Birkenau death camp, I
had traveled the globe with American presidents for more than a
decade. I had supervised the essential background details of summit meetings for three American presidents who had sought to
avert war and promote basic human understanding.

I relished the gamesmanship and the tensions, and my closeness to great and positive events; I was extremely proud of my work
and of America.

That ten-day trip to Poland would for me become a dark monument to the futility of such attempts.

I loved my work and would continue doing it enthusiastically
for another four years, but the Poland trip gave me pause.

I had flown into Krakow days before, working as what the
advance team called "the site man." My job was to assure that

things ran smoothly when the American delegation led by Vice President Dick Cheney arrived at the Auschwitz-Birkenau Memorial and Museum for the sixtieth anniversary of its liberation by the Red Army in 1945.

From my hotel in Krakow, I spent ten days making the short drive to the memorial, now preserved and open to visitors, who flock to the site from all over the world. I had made many such drives, attending to countless details for summit meetings and bilateral conferences attended by Presidents Ronald Reagan, George H. W. Bush, and his son, George W. Bush.

That drive was starkly different. Instead of concentrating on the details ahead that I needed to corral, I was filled with foreboding, struggling to control a visceral resistance to spending any time in a place of such unspeakable evil.

My fourteen-hour days would end with me standing atop a set of stairs between what had been two crematoriums on the memorial site. I would stare down at the steps where so many innocent human beings had walked to their deaths. I was drawn there, unable to digest the horror. I was not prepared.

* * *

The memorial service would be attended by more than a thousand survivors and the leaders of some forty countries, including our own delegation and others from Poland, Israel, Russia, France, and Germany.

Twenty years later it still haunts me.

My own dark tour of the two camps covering more than forty acres was a haunting reminder of how easily evil can insert itself into daily life. For me, it was numbing, incomprehensible. As I prepared for the ceremony, I walked slowly through rooms filled with the shorn hair of victims. I saw towering piles of eyeglasses and rooms of luggage so efficiently taken from the one and a half million men, women, and children who died there. I stared at the crematoria and the horrid dormitories from which workers left for the factories each day to perform the slave labor demanded of them by their Nazi captors.

On my daily rounds I would regularly pass the infamous sixteen-foot-wide wrought-iron sign bearing the words *Arbeit Macht Frei* ("Work makes one free"), under which prisoners would pass each day to and from their brutal work, the appalling cynicism of its creators nauseating to me.

Until that trip, I had never appreciated the degree of suffering inflicted on so many.

At the ceremony itself, after my work was finished and I became an observer, I would hear a camp survivor relate to the large gathering of world leaders how he had seen his father gassed, and how he himself had been tortured by the Nazis.

He spoke of the moment, of the overpowering symbolism of the gathering, and of his frustration.

"The message today is: 'No more Auschwitz.' But the world has learned nothing so far—you see they are fighting and killing each other everywhere in the world. Today they are saying a lot because of the anniversary, but tomorrow they will forget."

I could not have agreed more.

Auschwitz-Birkenau remains a stark reminder to me of the impotence of diplomacy, the very thing I had spent so many years helping to promote. The memorial is a paralyzing demonstration of the folly of world leaders, self-interest, and war itself. More than anything it speaks loudly to the very human tendency to avert one's eyes from things too dark to understand.

Thinking about that trip even now, almost twenty years later, I'm overcome by its power and the overwhelming sadness of that camp, the final resting place of more than a million and a half innocent human beings killed by the Nazis during World War II. It is a solemn warning about the basest of human impulse, and of hatred couched in political necessity.

For me it was a stark reminder of how power and insanity and political force can so easily produce what the German writer Hannah Arendt termed the "banality of evil." Auschwitz-Birkenau is an indelible and horrible reminder that human beings have an innate ability to see darkness and horror and look the other way if it does not affect them personally.

I did my job preparing for the meeting very well. Everything went according to schedule, our leaders were protected and safe, and the entire advance team was efficient and accommodating. I had no complaints from anyone—usually a good sign at the end of a trip. From a purely operational perspective, it was a good trip.

But I will never place the word "good" anywhere near that haunting memorial. Thinking about it now, I wonder how I managed. I spent the entire time at the memorial lost in a somnolent grief, surrounded by the silent voices of the men, women, and children killed so violently and casually and efficiently by the Nazis.

I knew that finding a faint sliver of irony, some small moment of ridiculousness, was the only way to stop myself from turning off the lights and crying.

That George W. Bush did not attend the ceremony was perhaps another reminder that such events, conceived in a perhaps futile hope that such cataclysmic horror does not happen again, is possibly another indication that such things are easily forgotten.

The world's press attended and wrote movingly of the ceremony. But there was a small subset who chose instead to focus on Vice President Dick Cheney's attire at the solemn remembrance on January 27, 2005.

I might have had a hand in what the vice president chose to wear that day.

My job called for managing the site—arranging seating and hotel accommodations; coordinating security, transportation, schedules, and the individual demands of a group among whom egos were always oversized. By then I had grown used to juggling the avalanche of minutia. That was my job.

But on that trip, the details I thrived on arranging seemed impotent, trivial beyond my comprehension. In the presence of such darkness, how was I supposed to robotically assure a VIP that his limousine would be roomy and comfortable, his hotel room large, and his flights on time? It was the only time in my twenty-year career that I felt trivial. I wanted to scream.

The biggest elephant in the room was the vice president. Dick Cheney was not a healthy man. By the time he attended the memorial service, he had survived four heart attacks. He would have another in 2010 and would undergo a heart transplant in 2012.

The weather for the ceremony was expected to be atrocious, the ceremony long, and the accommodations for attendees spartan.

Though I did not expressly state it, Cheney's health was behind a memo I wrote to the lead advance, Bob Athey, and to Ken Fairfax, the deputy chief of mission, the second in charge of our embassy in Warsaw.

January 21, 2005

Re: Managing Expectations re: January 27 Ceremony at Birkenau

I feel compelled to describe what we are likely to face at Birkenau on the 27th so that Washington knows what we are getting into before the delegation departs for Poland.

WEATHER CONDITIONS

On January 27 our delegation is going to face weather conditions that will challenge the mettle of even the strongest and fittest of us. Current weather forecasts place the temperatures at 17–20 degrees Fahrenheit. It will feel much colder when you factor in wind chill from 14 mph cold winds blowing from the northwest. The temperature at the Auschwitz Birkenau concentration camps is usually 10 degrees lower than ambient temperature. There are no windbreaks, hills, buildings, or geographical features to stop winds. There is no means of heating or other amenities—There are NO warming tents, hold rooms, or bathrooms. Heads of delegation will be expected to remain in their seats from the time of arrival until their departure two and a half hours later, with only a few minutes of movement when they are escorted a few yards to a plaque, where they will light a candle, and then to a guest book where they will sign their names. Auschwitz-Birkenau survivors, some of whom are in their 80s and 90s, are expected to stay seated throughout the ceremony. Other VIP participants, including our ambassador, will have to stand in one place during the entire ceremony.

ACCESS

We still need permission to get our motorcade as close to the ceremony site as possible. And as a special note, as of now our delegation will have to disembark at a security checkpoint and walk over 1,000 yards of rough terrain, which could be muddy or icy. Our success will depend on the generosity of our Polish hosts, who are also juggling the requests of 40 other delegations. We still have no confirmation how many vehicles and what type we can bring. Seating at the ceremony site has not been confirmed for Chief of Staff Libby, Liz Cheney, and her daughter Kate. Today in Warsaw, our embassy is trying to obtain seats through the ceremony organizers. If we cannot obtain those seats, we recommend direct intervention by the Ambassador.

We continue to press for whatever comforts we can obtain. We understand that hats, earmuffs, heavy coats, and scarves will not be out of place, and we advise all our participants to wear them. We are procuring 55 single-use chemical heating packs for VIP members of our delegation that they could conceal in their pockets, coats, socks, and footwear that should be able to provide some comfort during the ceremony; this amount will not be sufficient for all those who will be participating.

Cheney's attire at the ceremony, an olive-green US Air Force parka with a fur-trimmed hood and hiking boots, prompted ridicule from a fashion columnist at the *Washington Post*. The column was picked up by the wire services and television networks and took on a life of its own.

I dealt with the press frequently and respected them, even admired their doggedness. Respecting the press, ingratiating myself to them, of course, was prudent in my line of work. It was a way to encourage favorable coverage.

But the *Washington Post* column on Cheney's wardrobe irritated the hell out of me.

At yesterday's gathering of world leaders in southern Poland to mark the 60th anniversary of the liberation of Auschwitz, the United States was represented by Vice President Cheney. The ceremony at the Nazi death camp was outdoors, so those in attendance, such as French President Jacques Chirac and Russian President Vladimir Putin, were wearing dark, formal overcoats and dress shoes or boots. Because it was cold and snowing, they were also wearing gentlemen's hats. In short, they were dressed for the inclement weather as well as the sobriety and dignity of the event. The vice president, however, was dressed in the kind of attire one typically wears to operate a snow blower.

I felt it was a cheap shot, inappropriate and entirely devoid of useful commentary, given Cheney's fragile health and the purpose of the ceremony. It was a lazy response to low-hanging fruit.

I must admit, though, that Cheney had done himself no favors.

The week before, in a snowy Washington, Cheney had sat outside in the chilled air to attend the second inauguration of George W. Bush and his own swearing-in as vice president, dressed in only a formal overcoat—sans parka or woolen ski cap for protection.

After the Auschwitz ceremony, pundits were quick to point that out. I loved politics. I was energized by the game, well read, philosophical, and pragmatic about my choices. In my job I avoided politics by necessity. It was a survival technique I learned early. Don't jump into the fight. Do your job and move on.

I did wince at my role in the fashion debacle, though.

I felt Cheney redeemed himself in Poland, but it was in a little-covered address to a forum of world leaders in Krakow before the ceremony, with a moving speech that essentially went unnoticed in the coverage of his fashion misstep.

He stressed the importance of confronting evil before it takes hold:

> The story of the camps remind us that evil is real and must be called by its name and must be confronted. We are reminded that anti-Semitism may begin with words but rarely stops with words and the message of intolerance and hatred must be opposed before it turns into acts of horror.
>
> On this day in 1945, inside a prison for the innocent, liberators arrived and looked into the faces of thousands near

death—while miles beyond the camp, many thousands more were being led on a death march in the winter cold.

Inside barbed wire and behind high walls, soldiers found baths that were not baths, hospitals meant not to heal but to kill, and the belongings of hundreds of thousands who had vanished.

The ceremony itself was moving. It lifted my sagging spirits and injected, if only momentarily, a sense of optimism.

I listened intently as speakers talked of the horrors of the camps. One—ironically, given today's state of the world—was Russian President Vladimir Putin.

Elderly Holocaust survivors, some wearing tags with their prison numbers, sat stoically, wrapped in blankets in the blowing snow. For me it was an emotional testament to the strength of the human spirit, of its ability to survive and never lose hope.

Israel's president, Moshe Katsav, told the gathering, who knew only too well, "It seems as if we can still hear the dead crying out."

At day's end, I was spent, emotionally exhausted. Then, as I always did, I returned to Washington to await my next assignment and was soon reminded that some lessons are easier listened to than absorbed.

Over the next month, I would read the headlines. In a few short weeks in February 2005, they rolled along:

Five were killed in Egypt in a clash between security forces and suspects in a holiday bombing aimed at Israeli vacationers. A United Nations report outlined the killing, torture, and rape of civilians in Sudan's Darfur region and called for the perpetrators to be tried for war crimes. An unveiled secret report on the American base in Guantanamo Bay, Cuba, detailed abuse of prisoners.

German President Horst Kohler told the Israeli Knesset that his country needed to step up its fight against anti-Semitism.

A court in Guatemala halted a trial against sixteen military officers accused of war crimes.

An American congresswoman announced a bill to ban torture by Americans of the growing number of detainees captured in George W. Bush's War on Terror.

Six Rwandans filed suit in a French Court accusing French soldiers of complicity in the Rwandan genocide.

Former Bolivian president Gonzalo Sánchez de Lozada and his cabinet were formally charged with genocide.

The former commander of the Bosnian Army announced he will turn himself over to a UN tribunal for a trial in which he was accused of war crimes against ethnic Serbs.

In Mexico, the Supreme Court rules that former president Luis Echeverria cannot be tried for genocide because the thirty-year statute of limitations has expired.

Three British soldiers were convicted of abusing Iraqi prisoners.

And so it goes.

I moved on. There were more summits to attend, more issues for the leaders of the world to discuss.

CHAPTER 2

Managing the Invasion

I AM BY NATURE AN OPTIMIST.

My family and friends will tell you that I don't wear pessimism well. However, to succeed in supervising diplomatic excursions on the national and world stage for Presidents Ronald Reagan, George H. W. Bush, and George W. Bush, I needed to develop a sense for imagining the worst that could happen.

The world was watching.

For the twenty years that I oversaw many of these trips, I learned to conjure the type of dark creativity that saw disaster in every possible scenario.

In summits and private meetings with prime ministers and popes and the Queen of England—during tense interludes where the threat of war hung in the air, in peace, and in the anxious atmosphere that accompanies any international meeting—world leaders sought advice or tried to gauge American intentions.

There was no better way to learn than to speak with a president.

The task of keeping a president from embarrassment—or worse—on the world stage was like building a house of cards in a heavy wind. If one carefully placed card goes down, weeks of planning go with it.

Wherever he appears, an American president is an actor onstage under the brightest of klieg lights. His actions—a handshake, a smile, a tilt of the head, a joke or a jibe, his body language, what he says or doesn't say—are studied by allies and enemies alike. Those observers are reading the tea leaves for answers about what the most powerful country in the world is up to.

The most subtle stumble under such international scrutiny is magnified a hundredfold. A presidential gaffe is blood dripping into a pool of piranhas. Inevitably, a feeding frenzy ensues. For some observers looking for a weak spot, presidential mistakes serve as confirmation of darker motives from a country they view as having been too long at the top. A presidential misstep is Tom Brady throwing an interception or Babe Ruth striking out. It is newsworthy far beyond its actual importance.

My job was to prevent such frenzies.

Attention has been focused on American presidents' actions overseas since Theodore Roosevelt became the first American president to make a state visit in November 1906 to the Panama Canal and Puerto Rico.

My job did not entail simply managing the president. That would have been a cakewalk. On any overseas trip by an American president, hundreds of assistants and aides and hangers-on who accompany such a trip bask in the bright lights, enthralled by the sheer enormity of the power and influence they have attached themselves to.

My job—enthralling, nail-biting, nerve-wracking, and ultimately fulfilling—called for directing these wild cards as best I could, trying to keep these people on script when they were inclined to ad lib. Summoning the resources to make the trip successful and error-free was a job worthy of Sisyphus.

In my tensest moments, I often felt I was the only passenger aboard the *Titanic* who knew enough to worry about the iceberg. Around me, everyone else danced blissfully to their own music.

I knew international embarrassment lurked behind every presidential misstep or misstatement. I knew adrift, somewhere, was the iceberg, waiting for an opportunity to inflict chaos.

Everything a president or high government official does is noticed.

I worked closely with representatives of the foreign governments we visited, and with security teams including our own masterful Secret Service, to draw up plans that would minimize the potential for physical harm. I acted as a human Rosetta Stone, interpreting the cultural differences that could create an unintentional insult. I worked cautiously with an often-antagonistic media to put my man in the best possible light, literally and figuratively. I had to keep each president hovering safely above the flickering flame waiting to consume him.

I loved my job.

Throughout the history of American leadership overseas, there have been great triumphs, embarrassment, and danger.

In 1958, then Vice President Richard Nixon's motorcade was violently attacked in Caracas, Venezuela. Nixon could have been killed. I would see echoes of that Nixon trip when I arranged a trip for George W. Bush in 2002 to Lima, Peru, where a bomb planted by the infamous Shing Path guerrillas exploded four blocks from the American embassy. American Secret Service agents were, as always, in control and knew what to do. Actual presidential protection was not in my bailiwick, but I was charged with motorcade assignments, among other myriad details that could put the president in danger.

There have been other presidential incidents that sparked international attention, and usually not the best type.

Franklin Delano Roosevelt drew worldwide attention after he served hot dogs to the king and queen of England on their state visit in 1939.

At the Democratic National Convention that would nominate Harry Truman for president in 1948, organizers released dozens of doves into the stifling convention center in Philadelphia. Some of the doves died in their cages in the heat; others, struggling to escape the pandemonium, dive-bombed the delegates.

In a 1960 presidential debate in front of an estimated eighty million viewers that ushered in the Television Age and announced its unrelenting power, a gaunt and sweating Richard Nixon appeared no match for a tan and smiling John F. Kennedy.

On a state visit to Austria in 1975, Gerald Ford tumbled down the steps of Air Force One. Ford claimed an old football injury was the culprit, but that fall and others led to Ford's growing national reputation as a klutz.

In 1977 the ill-advised hiring of a hapless translator led to Jimmy Carter telling his Polish audience he was happy to grasp at their private parts. In 1979, on a much-photographed fishing trip to his hometown of Plains, Georgia, Carter swung a paddle frantically at a swamp rat trying to board his boat—an act that was promptly broadcast nationwide. The incident prompted a week's worth of national media coverage—and some critics to call Carter's actions "cowardly."

Ronald Reagan, much to the delight of his critics and the chagrin of his advisors, was photographed falling asleep on a visit with Pope John Paul II in Rome in 1982.

In 1992 George H. W. Bush vomited on Japanese Prime Minister Miyazawa Kiichi.

In a televised 2000 presidential debate between Democrat Al Gore, the sitting vice president, and George W. Bush, an exasperated Gore sighed so frequently at Bush's remarks that Republican campaign officials spliced each sigh into a seamless video reel and circulated it. It gave the appearance that Gore was aloof and disengaged. Gore was skewered by columnists.

In 2005 George W. Bush, taking a bicycling break from his duties at the G8 Summit in Scotland, lost control of his bike and ran over a policeman.

In 2008, at a press conference in Baghdad, an irate Iraqi journalist removed his shoes and threw them at George W. Bush in an odd and much interpreted incident viewed by millions worldwide. The journalist was highly praised for his efforts in the Arab world.

A haircut by a fashionable Hollywood stylist that Bill Clinton arranged on a quick Air Force One stopover at Los Angeles International Airport shut down two runways—a move that resulted in an estimated cost to airlines of $76,000, and led to pundits calling the presidential jet "Hair Force One."

On the face of it, these sorts of presidential incidents would be called minor and passing if they had involved normal citizens. To me, they were the stuff of nightmares. These were the very types of incidents I was charged with avoiding.

A multilateral meeting that I coordinated in June 2003 in Évian, France, spoke to another of my banes. Coordinating the typically heavy footprint of the American presence added angst to countries that were unprepared to accommodate the storm.

Meeting in Évian with George W. Bush were, among others, the heavy hitters of international diplomacy—Prime Ministers Jacques Chirac of France, Tony Blair of Great Britain, and Silvio Berlusconi of Italy, who were accompanied by discreet delegations.

The Americans were by far the largest delegation—a college marching band at a dignified string quartet recital in a small concert hall.

We flew in two 747s and accompanying support planes bringing in the presidential limousine and vehicles, dozens of helicopters, hundreds of support staff—people I grew to call "straphangers"—to the bucolic town on the shores of Lake Geneva. With us were the usual horde of press and the necessary tons of baggage for everyone involved.

Needless to say, my French counterpart was not pleased.

That was how we operated. I just had to deal with it.

By then I had immersed myself in what proved to be an intense graduate-level course in managing events. It was an interesting learning process for a job I was unaware existed in 1979 when I offered to help George H. W. Bush get elected president. He had a long road ahead of him and a popular opponent, Ronald Reagan.

The unpredictable eddies of presidential politics would propel me to Évian and beyond.

CHAPTER 3

Secrets

AT SUMMIT MEETINGS ESPECIALLY, WE HAD A BASIC AND INCON-trovertible need for safe places to talk.

Bureaucrats love acronyms, and on advance assignments none was more beloved or used more frequently than the one we applied to "sensitive compartmental information": SCIF.

These sealed and highly secure areas were impervious to eaves-dropping, electronic or otherwise. They were ubiquitous at summit meetings, and for good reason. People were listening, and often not with the best of intentions. If Ronald Reagan, George H. W. Bush, or George W. Bush needed to talk with a world leader outside the usual channels of a summit, we would set up a SCIF.

God knows, we needed them. Quite frequently, whether inten-tionally or through carelessness, rooms reserved by the host coun-try were usually in a hotel or conference center and had more leaks than a sieve—as more than one White House Communications Agency (WHCA) staffer told me.

The host would tell us everything was fine. The room is secure, they would say. Not taking them at their word—always a wise path—we'd scan the room, find the predicable listening devices, then set up a SCIF.

The White House advance teams I worked with became very efficient at setting up a last-minute SCIF.

Whenever I supervised creating a SCIF, watching as the WHCA team worked over a room, I would think back to my time in the army in the early 1970s, when my job centered on protecting facilities Americans used for a bit of listening of their own. We were as good at listening as the Russians, Chinese, or any other country wanting to know what rivals were up to.

In a foreign hotel room, helping set up a SCIF for a discreet presidential chat with another foreign leader, I'd think how little things had changed since 1970, when I enlisted and became a military policeman.

The year before I joined the army, 1969, had been an unsettled endcap to a tumultuous decade, years in which I had come of age. Richard Milhous Nixon would succeed Lyndon Johnson as president and become a lightning rod for a country growing increasingly rancorous over the war in Vietnam, racial strife, and generational misunderstanding.

In 1970 I had no idea that, a little more than a decade later, I'd be working for an American president.

In his inaugural address on January 20, 1969, Nixon would say that "Americans cannot learn from one another until we stop shouting at one another . . . the greatest honor history can bestow is the title of peacemaker. This honor now beckons America."

Oddly, considering I had a long career working for Republican presidents, before I enlisted, I had been working on Capitol Hill for liberal Democratic Senator Walter Mondale, the man Reagan would trounce in the 1980 election. Those years were formative for many of us.

For me, 1969 had many watershed events that today I recognize as exceptional. At the time they were important, but I did not see them as the truly significant milestones of change they were. History seems to work that way. American and North Vietnamese peace talks began in Paris. Mickey Mantle retired. Cleveland's Cuyahoga River caught fire. Neil Armstrong walked on the Moon, and, a little less than a month later, a music festival on a farm in Woodstock caught the country by surprise in upstate New York.

In Washington in June 1970, I knew I had an obligation to my country, and I knew that working for Walter Mondale was not fulfilling it. I enlisted in the US Army and soon enough found myself at Fort Dix, New Jersey, for basic training. From there I was sent on to Fort Gordon, Georgia, for military police school.

The US Army has a way of intuiting strengths, I suppose. Certainly, I did not go into the service knowing I had an aptitude that lent itself to the subtleties and nuances of security issues. At Fort Gordon, after I notched high scores on a round of tests, I was invited to join the Army Security Agency—an elite arm of the US Army.

The Army Security Agency was formed shortly after the end of World War II, in September 1945, and was charged with what was termed "signals intelligence"—a euphemism for intercepting, processing, and analyzing electronic communications of our adversaries.

Honestly, I would have been happy being a beat cop on a base, making my rounds and pounding a head or two in a rowdy bar if necessary. But such was not the case. And my time with the Army Security Agency would in turn provide me with experience in international relations and the darker world of intelligence gathering and the prevention thereof. It was one of those odd life twists. My education in the army, most specifically in Germany, where I would end up, gave me a leg up for my advance work—a job I had no idea existed at the time.

And a job I'd spend decades doing.

I began my education in the world of secrecy and clandestine services at Vint Hill Farms Station, in the horse country of Virginia near Warrenton, which is very close to where I live today, some fifty years later.

The seven-hundred-acre top-secret and highly secure facility was run by the Army Security Agency and its civilian partner, the National Security Agency (NSA). Vint Hill Farms Station conducted intelligence eavesdropping, including Soviet diplomatic and military communications. It also served as a base for training radio-intercept operators, cryptanalysts, and radio repair technicians.

To work there, I was vetted for and obtained a top-secret crypto clearance. I spent an interesting year there. In a tightly secured atmosphere, policing took on a higher meaning, with secrecy the currency of the day. The information collected at Vint Hill Farms Station was priceless at a time when we were deeply involved in a war in Vietnam, jousting daily with the Russians and Chinese.

The men and women stationed at Vint Hill Farms Station were, in many ways, the cream of the crop. They were intelligent, mentally agile, and more sophisticated than your average army draftee. They had been screened and tested and screened again to meet both the rigorous security clearances and intellectual standards to do the work they did.

While I worked and absorbed more training on the protocols of dealing with top-secret information and the people who handled it, I was still required to perform regular police work on the large campus. It was an odd juxtaposition. On one hand, there was the intrigue of watching over secret people dealing with potentially earth-shattering information. On the other, there was the day-to-day humdrum that no one would find in the latest James Bond movie.

We investigated traffic accidents and ticketed speeders. We handled domestic disputes and the normal confrontations that occur in any small town. The exceptional talents of the residents did not exempt them from human frailties.

There were moments of excitement, though.

I received a commendation for my diligence after I stopped a colonel from leaving the base with a briefcase holding classified material. We were required to search all bags leaving the station, and, colonel or not, I asked him to stop exiting the building on his way to the front gate and to open the briefcase he was carrying. I'm not certain if he had forgotten that the information was in the briefcase or if he had taken a chance the MP at the gate would not stop a full colonel.

After seeing what was in the briefcase, I asked him to step aside and then politely guided him into our guard shack, where I called the supervisor, who was also a colonel; then he was picked up by a security team and taken way. I never saw him again and did not learn the outcome of his interrogation. But I suspect it was not good.

This incident taught me to trust no one in the hall of mirrors that surrounded the taking of secrets, where no one was who they appeared to be.

I brought that lesson with me to my next assignment, another top-secret listening post run by the National Security Agency near Bad Aibling, Germany, a spa town about thirty-five miles southeast of Munch.

I was familiar with Europe. Following my opera-singing father had brought me to Holland growing up and to a stay in an English boarding school, where I had stood out and been bullied for being American.

My childhood had provided me with a gift to see beyond nationalities and look for the human spirit we all have in common. I had seen how cooperation and respect for other cultures and ways of doing things was better than closed minds and closed doors. The very real antagonisms and intrigues of the Cold War aside, I hoped I would have a chance to apply my philosophy.

The facility we guarded at Bad Aibling had begun its life as a Nazi airfield in 1936. After the war, the Army Security Agency took control, and by 1955 the facility had become a crucial Cold War listening center. When I arrived, it was still a major listening center, but under the control of the National Security Agency.

Bad Aibling was controversial. Some West Germans, acutely feeling the pressures of the Cold War, especially in a still-divided Germany, were not comfortable with Americans spying—and let's not split hairs, that is precisely what we were doing.

The listening post at Bad Aibling concentrated on Eastern Bloc countries, for example, Russian missile fields in Poland or transmissions as far away as Vladivostok. It was no secret. The Russians knew we were doing it, and we knew the Russians were doing the same thing to us. The difference, I suspect, was that Russia, then far behind Western technology, did not know how well we were doing it.

My arrival in Bad Aibling came at a fortuitous time. The National Security Agency had just taken control, and the entire Army Security Agency contingent was moved to Augsburg, West Germany—with one exception, forty-two military police, of which I was one.

That is where my philosophy of cooperation and understanding of the foreign countries we worked with would kick in, as did my luck. This would allow me to show that the Americans and West Germans had more in common than we had differences.

After another security upgrade, I was assigned to work with the West German police. I was fortunate to work for two stellar individuals who would become lifetime friends. The three of us worked very well together—myself, Phil Pease, who was director of NSA security for the base, and Sergeant Lloyd Kahler, my immediate supervisor.

My more-open philosophy, directly opposed to the more parochial and strongly held views of many Americans overseas that locals are to be avoided, if not completely shunned, would work wonders and reap many benefits.

Luckily, Pease and Kahler agreed with me.

I would use the same approach years later at every presidential summit meeting I was a part of.

My first foray into what I would call international relations came when I met Helmut Wycek, a sergeant on the local police force with whom I became good friends. Helmut would in turn introduce me to other local police. To me, it was a natural bond, two police forces with similar needs and common experience working together—God forbid, even helping each other.

It had never been done.

I spoke with Phil Pease about the potential symbiosis, how the two police forces could work to be mutually beneficial to each other. Phil jumped on board and encouraged me.

I started going out on patrol with the local force, and what an eye-opener that was, because it taught me how police—separated by thousands of miles, a language, and striking cultural differences—still had much in common.

I had not intended it, but our mutual work produced something else: trust. Soon enough, we began getting information from the local force on Americans living off post. Many of these guys were private contractors, experts in satellite technology or other hardware the NSA used to eavesdrop on the Soviets. These engineer types were making substantial salaries, as many government contractors did and still do.

They were often away from home on extended tours of several years. Temptations were high, and given what they knew about what the NSA was doing and how they did it, they were inviting targets for foreign intelligence services. It was a classic situation: Tempt someone with a woman or money, blackmail them, and force them to give up secrets.

This was not Ian Fleming, though. It was real life. And it happened frequently enough to be concerning.

Because of our cooperative work with the local police, we had eyes and ears on people we would not normally have access to. They were off base, so we had no way to monitor them ourselves.

Local police told me of an American contractor they had arrested after he had broken down the apartment door of his lover, a German woman. He had been teeteringly drunk. On one hand it was nothing more than a typical domestic fight. But given the man's job, his knowledge of classified information, and his weaknesses, he had to go.

I told Phil Pease. The man was on a plane home the next week.

We had another issue the local police helped us with. For some odd and unknown reason, groups of Romanian trucks would gather in a parking lot near the large antenna field used by the NSA for its eavesdropping. We'd often see clusters of these trucks, parked tightly together. They were outside the base, so there was nothing we could do to check.

I asked the local police to see what the Romanians were doing. As it turned out, nothing. The parking lot and the base were simply a convenient place to stop on long runs to and from Romania.

We stopped worrying.

The partnership worked both ways. We made our substantial gym available to the local police, who drop by to lift weights or play what became regular and spirited games of pickup basketball.

One of the things that still sticks with me, so simple, was an evening we opened the base bowling alley to the West German regional police and their families. They loved it and had what I could best describe as a lovely evening, with smiling kids and wives all around, Americans and West Germans.

It was an impressive sight.

Thinking back, that simple gesture could possibly have done more to bring two former enemies together that any summit meeting I worked for Ronald Reagan or the Bushes.

I'd finish my tour of duty and my army service in Bad Aibling. Back home I'd attend Franconia College in New Hampshire, earning a bachelor's degree in economics. My next step, I told myself, was to make my way up in the world of private business.

With the army behind me I was certain I was done with government work.

Chapter 4

Revenge Is Sweet

If I had the choice—a whimsical thought, I admit—I would have preferred to have been an advance man in the days when travel did not entail being inside an airplane at the mercy of the weather and of the mechanics and pilots who kept them in the air.

I like to have control over as many things as I can, and those elements are out of my hands.

Sitting on a bouncing airplane, jammed between fellow passengers thirty thousand feet above the ground, watching lightning shoot from the dark clouds the plane was passing through, never inspired confidence I was doing the right thing.

Those jarring flights made me think fondly of the days when Franklin Roosevelt or Herbert Hoover or Harry Truman did their campaigning on whistle-stop trains. What could go wrong there? Hit a few cows in Iowa maybe, but everyone except perhaps the cows would survive, and the campaign staff and advance people could go on to try to sway the opinions of voters.

I would not characterize my feelings about flying as hate, but it is close. A lot of the people I worked with knew of my unease. Still, over the course of my various careers, I have managed to accumulate more than a million miles aloft, in planes of all types and sizes. I'd have to say I have always managed my fears well.

One flying experience stands out, not because of its above-average terror factor, but because a certain colleague and his confederates in Washington thought that sending me on an early-spring flight along the western shore of Lake Michigan from Milwaukee to Iron Mountain, Michigan, would be a hilarious practical joke.

The jokester shall remain anonymous. My payback many months later was more than enough retribution for his underestimation of my ability to exact revenge. Naming him would be overkill and not, according to the tacit but unwritten rules of the practical joke game, sporting. I am satisfied I paid him back, and that will suffice.

Mind you, I have nothing against Milwaukee nor, for that matter, Iron Mountain, Michigan, my final destination. Getting out to the northern edge of the midwestern United States from Washington, though, meant taking several short but packed flights on boxy propeller-driven aircraft the Delta commuter lines used to reach off-the-beaten-path remote cities after I landed in Chicago. These planes usually offered no more than thirty seats, two rows on each side of a narrow center aisle, no in-flight amenities, and a good chance to be close enough to the engines to vibrate uncomfortably the entire flight. Usually the pilots looked only a year or two removed from getting their first driver's license. Conversation, something I was not inclined to indulge in anyway, was difficult over the roar of the engines.

At the time, I was doing advance work for Ronald Reagan's reelection campaign in 1984 and had already been across the country and back to Washington several times. To me, Iron Mountain, Michigan, though it seemed an odd place to expand campaign efforts, was just another stop.

My nameless colleague—the instigator of the joke—had told me in Washington that the event in Iron Mountain was "secret," a surprise press conference featuring Ronald Reagan's budget director, David Stockman. The media would be alerted shortly before I got to Iron Mountain, he told me. When I arrived, I would handle the conference, media, and other details.

Stockman had grown up in Michigan, received his undergraduate degree from Michigan State, and had served as a congressman from the state's fourth district in the 1970s. So the idea did not seem especially unusual. I suspected nothing untoward, though Iron Mountain seemed an odd venue.

The flight to Iron Mountain from Milwaukee was, to put it mildly, unpleasant. The 250-mile hop passes along the western shore of Lake Michigan and over Sturgeon Bay, bodies of water that in the early spring were roiled by departing winter winds.

It was on paper a short flight. To me it seemed interminable.

A four-year-old boy in the seat behind me began vomiting profusely and loudly shortly after takeoff, during which I swear the plane, buffeted by a strong gust of wind, turned sideways. My silent prayer and strained grip on both armrests as the plane dipped and yawed did nothing to relieve my discomfort. The young boy continued to heave as we reached cruising altitude. I began to wonder if his violent groans would be the last sounds I would hear in this earthly realm.

I had not enjoyed my flight to Milwaukee from Chicago. The flight to Iron Mountain was worse. A city of some seven thousand people tucked into the state's Upper Peninsula near the Minnesota border, Iron Mountain is known, its tourist brochures proclaim, for its Millie Hill bat cave, one of the largest artificial ski jumps in the world, and its bocce ball tournaments.

As I tried vainly to ignore the discomfort of the young boy behind me, I seriously questioned how crucial the city would be for Ronald Reagan's victory plans. It was not, in the argot of today's political world, a crucial "swing vote" city. A predictably ironclad Republican city, Iron Mountain would not be a major role player—nor, in fact, any sort of role player—in what would become Ronald Reagan's landslide victory in 1984.

As we bounced to a landing at Iron City's Ford Airport, the young boy seated behind me now blissfully silent, I was not happy.

I became even less happy—if that was even possible—when I learned my entire trip was the endgame of a practical joke.

I was told before I left Washington for the trip that there would be an envelope waiting for me at the Delta desk when I landed in Iron Mountain. Inside the envelope would be instructions on how to organize David Stockman's visit. At the time, Ford Airport had no jetway for passengers to walk directly into the tiny terminal. As I walked off the plane, my shirt soaked in perspiration, I said a silent prayer of thanks when my feet hit the tarmac.

I walked inside, spotted the Delta counter, walked over, and asked for the envelope.

The man behind the counter tried to stifle a grin, then reached into a drawer and handed me an 8 × 10 manila envelope with my name on it.

I opened it and pulled out a sheet of embossed White House stationery. I unfolded it and read: "Happy April Fool's Day from the Gang in Washington!"

I stood there, trying very hard not to swear or give any sign I was upset. I had been had, big-time. And I was steaming.

I took a deep breath and smiled.

"Ha! Good one," I told the crew behind the desk, who had obviously been filled in on the joke.

There was no David Stockman event in Iron Mountain, only a very angry advance man who had spent close to an entire day in airplanes to get there. And who would spend close to an entire day getting back.

As a master of the practical joke genre myself, once I calmed down, I had to tip my hat to its creator and his silent partners. Knowing my less-than-enthusiastic feelings about flying, they had created a plausible trip that called for a series of sketchy flights in the worst weather to a desolate destination on the lowest rung of campaign stops possible.

From a practical joker's perspective, it was genius.

What the jokesters—who no doubt had a good laugh about their prank—did not know was that they were toying with a master of the practical joke game. My strong suit was patience and deliberate calmness as I planned revenge.

Standing at the counter, I booked a return flight to Milwaukee on the same plane on which I had arrived. I could only hope they had cleaned the contents of the young boy's stomach from the seat-back he had spent the flight assaulting while I sat in front of him. I was clenching my teeth so tightly, my jaw began to hurt.

I called my wife, Gail, when I landed in Milwaukee and explained what had happened. Gail being Gail, she laughed uproariously. I would get no sympathy from those quarters.

My planning began on the flight back to Washington from Chicago.

My days as a military policeman had taught me a thing or two about the folly of acting rashly. I knew I needed time to plot, and I knew I needed to let a few months pass so my tormentors would think I had forgotten.

I had not. Trust me.

I took a deep breath and relaxed. I would exact revenge, and it would be sweet. When I got back to Washington, I congratulated my adversary for a job well done. In fact, I complimented him profusely on his cleverness and planning. I must admit, the extent to which he had gone did have something laudable to it.

But I knew I could do better.

I also knew I would have to wait, let the dust settle, and have my various enemies forget about Iron Mountain before I would act.

Then I would take the boy down.

In July 1984 I found myself in Sacramento for some survey work as the campaign entered its final months. It was a fortuitous assignment. California was not only home to Ronald Reagan and many of his top aides, it was also where the joker who sent me to Iron Mountain first cut his political teeth.

It seemed appropriate that I exact my revenge there.

My assignment called for three days of driving across the state to test the temperature of voters in five cities. I would be spending a lot of time in the car with a top aide to Governor George Deukmejian, Rick Davis, as well as a group of California Highway Patrol officers. The hours in the car gave me time to get acquainted with Rick, and we quickly became friends.

I told him about the Iron Mountain trip and its perpetrator, his fellow Californian, whom Rick had known through state politics. It seemed there had been some chafing in their earlier relationships.

It seems I had an ally.

"I can't believe he did that to you."

As soon as Rick said that, I knew California would be the centerpiece of my revenge, and with Rick's sympathy and his proximity to the governor's office, I knew I'd be able to pull off my plan.

With Rick's help, I got my hands on the various official State of California documentation I'd need to put my plan into action.

My tormentor was about to be named one of "10 Outstanding Californians" by the office of the governor.

I was not done.

The "official" notification the White House jokester would receive from the governor's office would also ask him to give the keynote speech at a late August banquet in Sacramento, announcing the awards after the Republican National Convention in Dallas.

We chose the date for the black-tie affair, and in separate press releases accompanying the invitation, we laid out a detailed schedule of pre-dinner press events and named the various media set to cover them. There would be print, television, and radio coverage, as well as a separate filmmaker, the release stated.

For my practical jokester in the White House, the man who thought it would be funny to send me for no reason to Iron Mountain, Michigan, it would be an occasion he could not miss—a deal anyone involved in politics could not refuse. The fact that it would be widely covered throughout the state was the icing on the cake.

The baited hook was set, and he took it without question.

I returned to Washington and said nothing more about my award-winning "10 Outstanding Californians" banquet to anyone.

On occasion I noticed when I passed by his office that my Iron Mountain man was studying index cards on which he had written his speech for the California awards dinner.

I said nothing.

Then I arranged for Rick Davis to put on the finishing touches on the evening of the "banquet."

Rick later filled me in on what happened.

My man arrived at the Sacramento hotel at which the gala was supposedly taking place, checked in, then changed into his tuxedo.

When he walked up to the closed door of the State Capitol building, a guard at the door welcomed him, coached by Rick Davis to say, "We've been expecting you."

Then, as he opened the door to the cavernous but empty rotunda, Rick handed him a note: "Welcome to Iron Mountain, California. Paybacks are a bitch."

Gail later made me a trophy featuring the invitation to the "10 Outstanding Californians" dinner and the note I had attached, which I later presented to him.

I'm certain he tossed it immediately.

Game. Set. Match.

Chapter 5

Challenging

IDEALLY, PLANNING FOR ANY PRESIDENTIAL APPEARANCE BEGINS months beforehand. Good lead times allow for soft landings and favorable responses. A presidential event of any kind is a simmering stew of competing forces, with cameras, reporters, and attention focused on one man and what he does and says.

The trick was to keep it from boiling over.

In the real world of politics and presidential influence, things are rarely ideal. When the normal time to plan is compressed, the heat rises for everyone involved.

The wrenching explosion of the space shuttle *Challenger* on January 28, 1986, shocked the entire nation. Americans had grown accustomed to flawless space shots. Millions saw the liftoff on television, among them excited schoolchildren watching from their classrooms that morning to cheer for New Hampshire schoolteacher Christa McAuliffe, who was among the crew of seven who perished when the *Challenger* disintegrated seventy seconds after liftoff.

Ronald Reagan postponed his State of the Union address that evening while the shocked country mourned. He would fly to the Johnson Space Center in Houston on February 1 to speak at a memorial service and to meet with the mourning families of the deceased astronauts.

The country was reeling, its collective confidence eroded. Nothing like that had ever happened in decades of celebrated space flights. It was a time of national sorrow and reckoning, and many needed Reagan's consoling words. He would speak to a gathering of some ten thousand mourners in Houston at an outdoor gathering at the Johnson Space Center.

We had a day and a half to prepare.

Even under the best of circumstances, there are always crosswinds in these complicated outings, and I learned to expect them. With the luxury of a month or two to read the currents and adjust, I could usually come up with ways to avoid surprises. I knew to expect problems, but I could never predict what direction they would come from, or what force they would exert.

One such gust came from Teddy Kennedy, a man accustomed to having his demands met promptly.

As we hastily arranged flights, press coverage, seating arrangements, and security, others in Washington began their own preparations. With the nation's eyes focused on this single event, many saw an opportunity to gain crucial political capital, the currency many members of Congress and my own so-called straphangers craved. The president and his wife, Nancy, and at least ninety members of Congress would make their way to Houston.

There was no better opportunity for national recognition than to bask in the president's reflected light. Elected officials, Republican and Democrat alike, state and national, would be in Houston seeking the attention such an event would bring. That fact was as predictable as the swallows returning to San Juan Capistrano. Even with thirty-six hours to plan, I knew it would happen.

The biggest problem was when someone would inject himself into my carefully laid plans, like parched men in the desert hoping for a drink of water.

The Reagans insisted that they meet privately with about twenty-five members of the astronauts' families before the president addressed the larger gathering. I had found Ronald Reagan to be easy to work for, voluble, easygoing, and always ready accept unexpected changes in plans—for me, a perfect attitude.

Nancy, on the other hand, was exacting. She knew what she wanted and expected us to accommodate her requirements. I learned quickly to obey, and to keep my distance.

Nancy insisted that only she and the president would meet with the families. Her insistence would not sit well with Senator Kennedy.

He had other plans. He wanted to meet with the astronauts' relatives. I stood in the way, and that would spark a vigorous exchange.

The senator approached me that morning with his nephew, John F. Kennedy Jr., and niece, Caroline Kennedy Schlossberg, in tow. They stood behind him sheepishly but said nothing as he began to fume.

"Are you the advance man?" he asked.

"I am, Senator," I replied.

"I need to speak to the families," he said.

"I'm sorry, Senator," I told him, "but only the Reagans will meet with the families. Mrs. Reagan insists."

My reply did not sit well. It had been an emotional day, with many tears. Senator Kennedy's prevailing emotion, however, was anger.

He stepped up, two inches from my face, and indelicately told me I was mistaken.

I held my ground, knowing the consequences of Nancy Reagan's wrath would be far worse than Kennedy's if I let him into the room.

Astounded, I'm sure, by what he saw as my insolence, Kennedy presented his trump card. Despite their political differences, Kennedy was good friends with Reagan's secretary of the treasury, Donald Regan, a Cambridge, Massachusetts, native and former US Marine known for his toughness.

"I'll have your job," Kennedy screamed at me, throwing in a choice expletive. "I'll give Don Regan a call, and you'll be gone."

I did not flinch. "You are not going in there."

The Reagans met with the families, and Senator Kennedy stood outside.

A week or so later, I mentioned my run-in with Kennedy to Regan.

He laughed.

I kept my job and became something of a folk hero among the support staff.

By the time Senator Kennedy was offering to assist me in losing my job, I was familiar with what in the trade is called "advance work."

* * *

In 1979 I became convinced that George Herbert Walker Bush would make a terrific president. I liked his style and his message and felt he would be an antidote to the growing voter malaise over what I saw as the ineffective policies of the Jimmy Carter administration. That year, Americans were beset by an energy crisis, with long lines at the gas pumps. Carter's efforts to reform the country's welfare, health care, and tax systems seemed to me to be failing, in part because he lacked influence in Congress.

George H. W. Bush was the antidote, I thought. He was a war hero. By then he had been a member of Congress from Texas, director of Central Intelligence, the chairman of the Republican National Committee, and chief of the US Liaison Office in the People's Republic of China. He was a popular and influential Washington figure who could get things done.

I offered to help him get elected.

My offer caught the attention of Roger Whyte, an influential Washington figure and Bush supporter who had been director of advance for Vice President Nelson Rockefeller and who would go on to serve as director of operations for the Bush campaign.

I felt we had the momentum and the support necessary to win the Republican nomination.

Only Ronald Reagan stood in the way.

In May 1979 I attended my first class in what would become a twenty-two-year career in advance work at the Crystal City Marriott in Arlington, Virginia, on the banks of the Potomac looking over Washington, a city I knew intimately. Though I had grown up in eclectic surroundings in Europe, the son of a concert singer, my family had owned the *Washington Evening Star*, a once influential and much read daily newspaper, for 114 years. There was no better or more intimate way to understand the intricacies of Washington politics than to hear about them over dinner.

I began my career in advance work as most people begin any career, at the bottom, arranging hotel rooms for the Bush campaign in the northeastern United States. Along the way, I began to learn about the ever-important task of massaging image. While a remarkable and approachable man, the patrician Bush was seen by many as too preppy, too disengaged from the daily lives of most voters. While he had served ably in many high-level positions, he was a raw candidate, and raw candidates are regularly eaten for lunch.

Sometimes the simplest thing can have immediate effect. We persuaded Bush to stop wearing his sweaters tied around his neck, a signature preppy style foreign to steelworkers in Pittsburgh or lobstermen in Maine.

Reagan, the former governor of California and a well-known Hollywood movie star, had a growing and enthusiastic base. He appealed to the populist nature of the voters, now disenchanted with Carter. His philosophy would later give rise to a powerful bloc of traditional blue-collar voters known as "Reagan Democrats."

His appeal was powerful, since he had also established himself as the choice of conservative Republicans.

George H. W. Bush had an uphill slog, and in the 1980 Republican primary he lost to Reagan, whose finely honed communication skills were simply too difficult to overcome.

All was not lost. I had enjoyed the Bush advance work, and Reagan and one of his top advisors, Michael Deaver, saw George H. W. Bush as a man who could bring in moderate votes from both parties in the crucial Northeast in the general election. Reagan chose Bush as his vice presidential candidate.

I was asked to serve on the team. I was still in the game, working under Stephen Stoddart, an astute advance man who would go on to organize Reagan's 1981 and 1985 inaugurals and be a trusted advisor during both of Reagan's terms.

One of my first jobs was press and hotel logistics for Reagan's 1980 debate in Cleveland. During walk-throughs, I got to know the Reagan people very well, Mike Deaver among them. I learned from Deaver a lesson I would adhere to for the next twenty-two years as I polished my trade. Deaver was the brains behind Reagan's advance: Stay on one message a week; do not stray. Keep to the point and stick to it. Unclear messages beget unclear responses.

I had not grasped the fact in my youth, but I had been preparing for the work of understanding the nuance of message and image and how the public interprets both since childhood. It was in my blood.

I grew up surrounded by journalists, with parents who stressed the value of reading and opening our minds as my father's career as concert baritone led us to Europe during the Cold War years that pitted East against West in the 1950s. At family meals we dined on politics and philosophy.

My great-great grandfather, Crosby Stuart Noyes, a native Mainer, published his first newspaper in Minot at age fifteen. He moved to Washington, DC, in 1847, so poor he had to walk from Baltimore because he lacked train fare. He worked in a bookstore, as a theater usher, and as a route agent for the *Baltimore Sun* before becoming a reporter for the weekly *Washington News*. In 1855 he became a reporter for the *Evening Star* and, in 1867, bought it with two partners.

Crosby Stuart Noyes would become close to Abraham Lincoln, and the paper grew in status during the Civil War and the years beyond.

My family would hold an interest in the paper until 1975. Considered a voice of the center right, its reporters would win ten Pulitzer Prizes, but it would cease publication in 1981.

As a young man, I had the privilege of listening to frank, informed conversations on the intricacies of world and national affairs by some of the nation's top journalists, including my uncle Smith Hempstone and his good friend Richard Harwood, a veteran reporter.

My uncle had worked as a reporter for the *Louisville Times*, as the Africa correspondent for the *Chicago Daily News*, and as a reporter for the *Washington Star*. He wrote several books and a syndicated column carried by ninety newspapers. He would later serve as US ambassador to Kenya.

His good friend Dick Harwood was a reporter and editor at the *Washington Post*, famed for his no-nonsense approach to news and how it should be reported.

Both were tough ex-Marines, my uncle during the Korean War and Harwood in World War II, where he took part in the bloody invasion of Iwo Jima. Both were realists who had worked their way up the hard way—and both held engaging worldviews forged by their shared experience.

My classroom was often my uncle's boat, the *Baracka*, as it made its way along the Choptank River off Chesapeake Bay. In my late teens, I served as a deckhand, sitting back unnoticed as the Jack Daniels and conversation flowed, just absorbing it all. Aunt Kitty Hempstone would be all over the boat—from being in the galley cooking for the group to popping up to the deck to ensure the conversation was civil.

Those cruises proved priceless to my education, which was furthered by my father, Garfield Christian Swift, a lyric baritone whose concert career led us around Europe while it was recovering from the devastation of World War II, aided by the brainstorm of Secretary of State George C. Marshall that bore his name. The Marshall Plan would provide $15 billion to help finance rebuilding efforts on the Continent. In a small way, my family was part of it. My mother, Elizabeth Ross Thompson Swift, as noted earlier, was a friend of Marshall's and worked as an office administrator when my father's career took us to The Hague, in the Netherlands.

My father spoke five languages, but one of his clearest messages to me was in simple English. I'd recall it often in my years as an advance man, surrounded by world leaders and the power they radiated: "Do not be maddened by your own perfume."

Don't get a big head, don't spend too much time admiring yourself or patting yourself on the back. It is all fleeting.

I would glean similar advice from watching George H. W. Bush, who was, above all things, the ultimate diplomat who abhorred hubris. He would always make a concerted effort to see his adversaries as they envisioned themselves. He thought before he spoke.

By the time I began my advance career, the essence of the job had been changed by the influence of one man, Ron Walker, Richard Nixon's director of advance. Walker pioneered the art of a franker, more intense approach to international relations that was less diplomatic.

He inaugurated his new philosophy when he supervised Nixon's trip to China in 1972, considered a watershed moment of Nixon's presidency. Walker had insisted that Nixon avoid political niceties. He advised Nixon to be forceful in his views that a partnership between the United States and Mao Tse Tung's previously inscrutable China would be beneficial, despite the huge differences in political goals.

Walker held that unless one proves ownership of his ideas, he is lost. "Be presidential," Walker insisted. "Be strong." Nixon agreed. A new era of somewhat harmonious relations ensued.

When I began advance work in 1979, Walker's influence had faded slightly; and as I stepped into running international presidential trips, I quickly realized I was now in a far more intense theater, where mistakes were amplified.

My first rule became "Don't make enemies." A corollary that echoed my father's earlier advice: "Stay in your lane." I knew my place, understood my job, and did not call attention to myself or my aides. I stressed the art of diplomacy.

I also learned a valuable lesson from Mike Deaver. Deaver stressed perspective. He told me to view any event I organized through the eyes of a reporter from the *Washington Post* or the *New York Times*.

Granted, I never became friends with reporters—we called them "the pencils"—but knowing that Ronald Reagan, George H. W. Bush, and George W. Bush were often viewed antagonistically by much of the larger national press proved essential. Viewing an event through their eyes proved valuable.

On the other hand, I quickly learned to become allies with the photographers. A strong image is often more important than a president's words. I would always ask myself, "What is going to make the president look good?"

I took photographers' advice on lighting and perspective and how to set up the best possible images, which would of course be viewed worldwide. I frequently sought advice, grabbing a photographer or news cameraman, pulling him inside the rope line before a president would speak.

"Should I move the dais?" I'd ask.

"Should I move the crowd up or back?

"Is this a good angle for you?"

I would accommodate them in any way they wanted, and, more times than not, they would reciprocate with strong images.

Photographers quickly became my allies. I was learning.

An ashen and visibly shaken Ronald Reagan spoke to the mourners in the bright sunlight of Houston. Many in the crowd were sobbing, moved by what became one of Reagan's iconic speeches. Photographers and television cameras captured the moment, and the images from that afternoon moved an entire nation.

By the time Teddy Kennedy was threatening to have me fired, I was a confident if unseen advisor. I was also confident that Teddy Kennedy's bluster would blow over quickly.

In the game of politics, though, one can be never be too sure.

CHAPTER 6

The Rope Line

THE UNSMILING MAN TWO FEET BEHIND MY RIGHT SHOULDER stood out from the jubilant throng. His silence, sunglasses, and the way he filled out his dark suit contrasted with the smiles and chatty group around me. As the motorcade approached, I heard "Gun!" and noticed a blurred figure to my left step over the rope line and raise his right hand, in it a pistol.

The unsmiling man behind me exploded from his stance, burst through the people unfortunate to be in his way, slammed the potential assassin into the pavement, and jammed his index finger into the very tight space between the hammer and firing pin of what was later identified as a Smith & Wesson Shield Plus.

It happened so quickly, I was unsure of what I had just witnessed.

My jaw dropped. It was an astonishing display of athleticism.

I had been taking part in what was called an "assault on the principal" drill. It had been painstakingly designed by the Secret Service to help me and others on presidential advance teams understand how a presidential appearance unfolds and the hidden terrors within. Over the years I would take part in many such drills. These exercises made it clear to me that my goal to put the president in the best possible light did not dovetail neatly with the Secret Service's goal of keeping him alive.

My advance colleagues and I wanted an uninterrupted stream of clear messaging, symbolism, and positive emotions from an adoring public. These are the oxygen of politics, the essence of elected office.

The Secret Service wanted only the president's safety.

The irreplaceable value of the razor-sharp reflexes and power I witnessed during that drill was brought horribly home to me on March 30, 1981, when Ronald Reagan came perilously close to being killed outside the Washington Hilton.

I was blocks away, not involved in the president's luncheon speech to representatives from the AFL-CIO.

I was shocked at the news, disturbed that it had happened at home, where, theoretically at least, things were easier to control. The assassination attempt did not happen during Reagan's speech but rather after the event, as he approached his limousine outside. The advance plans and logistics for Reagan's appearance inside the hotel ballroom that afternoon had flowed as planned.

Still, the attempted assassination gave every one of us on the advance team great pause. It emphasized the fragility of any public appearance, whether in Washington or Moscow or anywhere else on Earth.

I would learn later that the attempted assassin, John Hinckley Jr., had inserted himself, unchecked, into an area normally reserved for the press—something the Secret Service usually checks vigorously. The press always had the best access. Despite its heroics on March 31, the Secret Service had failed to properly screen the group, which stood that afternoon fifteen feet from the president, Hinckley among them.

Only the immediate response of the Secret Service saved Reagan's life. At the first sound of gunshots, the lead agent walking beside Reagan as he waved to the crowd grabbed Reagan's shoulders and dove with him through the open door of the waiting presidential limousine, assisted by a second agent.

A third agent put himself in the line of fire, blocking the open door. He was shot in the abdomen.

Despite these heroic actions, Reagan was hit by a ricocheting bullet under his left arm that broke a rib and punctured a lung. He was close to dying when he reached George Washington University Hospital, a little more than a mile way.

He would recover and be released on April 11.

White House Press Secretary James Brady was shot in the head, a grievous injury he would never completely overcome.

The days following the assassination attempt were grim for all of us, the advance teams and the Secret Service, our disparate goals suddenly gelling.

That near miss would change the way we planned events and our view of adhering to the edicts of the Secret Service. Political points gained by a successful appearance were abruptly muted.

Tension between the advance people and Secret Service was as predictable as a rising tide. We wanted color, and that meant smiling and enthusiastic people as close to the president as possible and, with them, photographers to capture the magic. The Secret Services wanted only safety. Both groups were not oblivious to the other's needs, and we worked with that in mind. We were realists.

I had always had paramount concern for safety, but I also loved opportunities for color, admiring faces, and bystanders enraptured by their closeness to history. Color is the essence of political life, but political life is quite different when seen from the wrong end of a gun held by someone filled with hate. I knew we needed to work closely with the Secret Service and respect their concerns.

Most concerns arose along the fragile line between a smiling president just yards away from an adoring public. That interface was the seismic fault line, where inattention could wreak horrendous results, where the tsunami of details the advance team laid out before an event could go south and utter chaos ensue. It was a nightmarish result no one wanted.

I developed my own philosophy, and it served me well over the years. The men on a presidential Secret Service team are big, athletic, and not given to friendly hellos or idle conversation. I was not inclined to pick fights with guys the size of refrigerators carrying .357 Magnums, but I had a job to do.

In a perfect world, I'd love to have photographers within twelve feet of the president, and the rope line holding back crowds within shouting distance to build excitement. The closeness made for intimate, empathetic photographs. Such intimacy did not sit well with the Secret Service, and for good reason. There was always tension between the advance people and the Secret Service, but there were always solutions as well.

Behind the rope were adoring admirers hoping to glimpse or even touch a president. The Secret Service could screen observers, but that only went so far. Anyone with ill intent and capable of the smallest talent for duplicity could make their way to the rope.

Reaching an agreement with the uncompromising Secret Service sometimes required the balance of a Wallenda. Driven by a common uncompromising interest in the president's health, solutions were usually close at hand. I made it a point that any discussion not become a future negative. If I butted heads with the Secret Service at a planning session or, on a rare occasion, on-site, I would always defer to my bosses at the White House or ask the agent to call his superiors. I did not want a face-to-face confrontation.

Kicking a decision upstairs proved to be the best way to settle a question.

Four US presidents have been assassinated: Abraham Lincoln in 1865, James A. Garfield in 1881, William McKinley in 1901, and John F. Kennedy in 1963. Those deaths are a morbid record I had no interest in adding to. They appalled me, and the thought that I could make a decision that could put any human being in harm's way, presidents included, put me on edge. I had those deaths in mind each time I planned a presidential visit.

There have been many close calls over the years, though the memories of what at the time were shocking have faded for the most part. Presidential candidate George Wallace, at a 1972 appearance in Laurel, Maryland, was shot and paralyzed for life when Arthur Bremer stepped from a crowd and shot him as the two were shaking hands. The Secret Service had advised Wallace against such close contact.

Lynette Fromme, a member of the infamous Manson Family, pointed a gun at President Gerald Ford during an appearance in Sacramento's Capitol Park before she was pounced on by Secret Service agents in September 1975.

Andrew Jackson in 1835, Theodore Roosevelt in 1912, Franklin Roosevelt in 1933, and Harry Truman in 1950 all escaped assassination attempts.

I took my drills and my preparation very seriously. I insisted that the thick binder I prepared for staff before an overseas trip be mandatory reading. My prep meetings, perhaps not enthusiastically, were known for their length. I tried to leave nothing unconsidered.

The Secret Service did its own painstaking research, which was essential and eminently helpful to my own planning. I respected them, and they made my job not only less nerve-wracking but also easier. Though we sometimes disagreed on process, we had the same goal in mind.

One small example of the level of detail I injected for a visit by George W. Bush to the 2003 G8 Summit in Évian, France, might provide a snapshot. I visited the area a month before to get the lay of the land and distributed my report to everyone who would be attending. All overseas trips are an exercise in redundant caution, an overkill of sorts that I was entirely comfortable with.

I always assessed the general security situation, a broad view of potential trouble. Then I would compile a report to alert every team member on what to expect and, most important, what to be aware of.

Potential problems lurked even along the bucolic shores of Lake Geneva in Switzerland, where the president would land before crossing to Évian. As enticing as such a trip would seem, it was no vacation.

In a sensitive document I distributed to my staff, I included the following information:

"An uncertain security situation around Lake Geneva and Lausanne portend potentially major problems for the Geneva arrival on June 1 and planned rapid transfer to Évian."

I added, "The overall security situation in Geneva remains uncertain. While difficult to predict exact numbers of demonstrators, police sources and others estimate 30,000 to 50,000 as realistic numbers. Swiss newspapers routinely use estimates of 100,000 to 300,000. There is widespread concern about the lack of sufficient Swiss police resources to deal with unexpected demonstrators and the range of G8 security needs."

There would be very few if any rope lines for that visit, nor were there any plans for intimate photos of adoring crowds.

I made sure advance plans, despite our occasional spats, dovetailed neatly with those of the Secret Service. My status as an army veteran and former military policeman gave me some purchase with the agents, a bit of respect. My inclination and affection for dialectics—for having a civil discussion and coming to a logical conclusion—always held sway. The Secret Service agents I dealt with bought into that.

I learned that very clearly on an advance trip to Hamtramck, Michigan, in 1992 to review plans for a speech by George H. W. Bush, the incumbent president in a tight race against Bill Clinton and H. Ross Perot. Hamtramck was a meat-and-potatoes city. It was a former Democratic stronghold in a state whose political tastes were changing. Ronald Reagan had won in Michigan in 1980 and 1984, and it was where Bush won in 1988 over Democrat Michael Dukakis. Hamtramck held the type of voters Bush needed, and the advance team wanted color and access and persuasive photos and newsreels of enthusiastic voters, who frankly were not drawn to the patrician Bush.

I visited the site with agent Lew Merletti, a Vietnam war hero who would go on to lead the Secret Service. Over the years, Merletti would work for Gerald Ford, Jimmy Carter, Ronald Reagan, George H. W. Bush, and Bill Clinton; he was named special agent in charge of Clinton and his family.

Merletti knew what he was doing.

I knew Bush needed smiling throngs and thought a speech in a park in the center of town would provide an ideal setting. Merletti thought otherwise. We walked the area, Merletti offering commentary on the park that I felt was an ideal location. Merletti pointed to the buildings surrounding it.

It was not a good idea, he told me. Too many older buildings with sight lines to the park, with windows that opened. He did not tell me to move the proposed speech to an area where agents would have more control. He merely pointed out the negatives. There were many. I did not insist that park was the only place we could have the speech.

We talked it through, calmly and logically.

We learned later that a man who had been stalking the president around the country was in Hamtramck and had planned to assassinate Bush.

My sensitivity and respect for the Secret Service, already heightened, increased. They do, after all, hold a well-deserved reputation as the world's best dignitary protection service. That would be brought home repeatedly to me over the years as I participated in assault on the principal drills. It was during one such drill that I saw the athletic agent spring into action to jam the potential assassin's handgun with his finger.

The drills, to say the least, were instructive, and the main lesson was "Get out of the way."

Participants would stand along the rope line as a motorcade slowly passed by, the presidential limousine's open windows, the presidential stand-in waving vigorously within feet of us.

Without warning, a sharp and clear "Gun!" would ring out. As advance people, we were always nearby, often on the rope line, our eyes on the president, ears alert for anything untoward. But we were neither trained nor athletic enough to do anything physical to help the situation.

Our duty was to get out of the way.

If we did not act quickly enough, an agent would help us do so, usually by knocking us to the ground if we were in the way. The drills were not designed by Emily Post, and the only etiquette demanded was to not complain as we picked ourselves up off the asphalt.

Over the years, after a few early ground-level close-ups of curbs and skinned knees, I learned to get out of the way—very quickly.

Knowing that the Secret Service is very serious about its duties provided some small sense of security as I planned the next presidential outing.

CHAPTER 7

An Elephant Never Forgets

IN 1979 I HAD A FULL-TIME JOB I LOVED. I HAD NO PLANS TO leave it.

I volunteered to work, unpaid, for George H. W. Bush because of my innate interest in politics and my desire to see him in the White House. I felt he would be the best candidate to set a new course to correct Jimmy Carter's flawed policies. After Ronald Reagan named Bush as his running mate, I continued as a volunteer during the general election.

My employer was gracious enough to let me indulge my interests, with the understanding that I'd be back to work once the election was over.

I knew my contributions were minor on the grand scale of things, but helpful. I wasn't looking for a job, nor did I expect my efforts would lead to a new career.

When I offered to help Ronald Reagan and George H. W. Bush during the Republican primary, I was an executive for the Stouffer's hotel chain, handling sales for its popular property in Crystal City, Virginia—a tight and growing complex of underground shopping malls and connected buildings that housed many of the country's leading defense contractors, among other firms tied to the area's chief industry: government business. Technically a suburb of Arlington, Crystal City was a stone's throw across the Potomac from Washington, DC, and less than a mile and a half from what was then known as National Airport.

By then I had developed a knack for knowing the ingredients necessary to smooth the ragged edges brought on by too much travel in too short a time. I knew what jaded travelers needed, and I knew how to attract attention to what Stouffer's had to offer. It was a great job.

By 1980, presidential campaigning meant crisscrossing the country with little sleep, eating rubber chicken after speeches and fried dough at state expos, washed down by gallons of coffee. I'd seen plenty of that on the road with the George H. W. Bush campaign.

I knew a campaign diet was enough to make a cardiologist blanch. One can force down only so many pigs in blankets, cheese fries, and county fair corn dogs. Anyone on the road with a candidate—the press, advance people, aides—had to have cast-iron stomachs and the internal strength to eat and gird themselves for the next stop and the next culinary onslaught.

I also knew from my brief time on the road and from talking to other more seasoned campaigners that sneaking catnaps on campaign buses and planes was not the recommended path to developing goodwill toward others, especially after a few weeks, when each stop begins to look the same.

I had learned from my job as general sales manager for Stouffer Hotels and Resorts that a quiet and spotless air-conditioned hotel room, starched and clean sheets, and perhaps a private bar could seem like an oasis for weary, frazzled travelers.

By the time Ronald Reagan asked George H. W. Bush to join him as his vice presidential candidate, I had gained a reputation as "the hotel guy."

For hardened campaigners, I became a touchstone for the illusive comforts they sought—the magical aide who knew how to find the spacious beds in quiet rooms and the amenities that could provide some small amount of respite from the grind. A good meal and a great night's sleep, cable television, coffee maker and microwave, and a well-stocked minifridge during an interminable campaign was manna from heaven. A quiet room can be more precious to a benumbed candidate and his large posse of haggard aides than a new speech or a policy epiphany.

I knew that after a week or so of dubious motels offering vending-machine sandwiches of questionable pedigree and stale candy bars, the Stouffer's in Crystal City looked heavenly. I knew also that it was convenient for the politicos who returned to Washington frequently, landing at National Airport.

By then, I also had learned to stay in my lane.

I was not about to pitch the Stouffer's in Crystal City as the perfect antidote for the ragged Reagan campaigners. That was not what I had signed up for. By complete chance, though, I was given the opportunity to do just that—and it changed my entire career arc.

It is not as if there is a university degree for advance people, but I learned very quickly that to be effective I had to catch the attention of the right people. I knew I had to show the ability and agility to manage a torrent of details and keep many people happy. Something as seemingly inconsequential as a quiet room and maybe a little wine and cheese or a cold beer in the minifridge could win a lot of hearts and minds.

When I volunteered to help the Bush campaign—and many of the advance staff were unpaid volunteers—I thought I would simply step away from Stouffer's, help out, then return to my job when the campaign was over.

When Ronald Reagan asked George H. W. Bush to serve as his vice president, I was one of only a few Bush people to be asked to stay on. My bosses at Stouffer's allowed me to extend my time away from the office. At the time, I did not know my efforts would lead me to center stage at history-making events, surrounded by world leaders.

As "the hotel guy," I had become a sort of patron saint of travel, the guy to turn to for a good night's sleep on the road, a master of amenities. I understood the art of keeping travelers happy, and happy people are grateful people.

As the campaign ramped up, the Reagan people would fly into National Airport then disperse. Reagan and his top aides would quickly head out to an estate in Middleburg in Virginia's lush horse country, a forty-five-minute drive from the airport. Neither Reagan nor his top aides were interested in hotels.

Regular staff did not have such luxurious alternatives to consider. Most would stumble off the plane, fight for cabs or negotiate the new metro system to head into town, slowly negotiating the usual dense Virginia traffic to reach a Sheraton they had been using regularly. Ronald Reagan was likely at his Virginia country retreat before many of his staffers were unpacking at the Sheraton after their usual slog from National Airport. Then they would unpack and try to find a place to maybe get a drink and something to eat.

They were underwhelmed by the arrangements.

One afternoon Michael Deaver's top aide, Shirley Moore, pulled me aside.

"I understand you're a hotel man. What can you do to make things easier?"

I had apparently caught the attention of the right person. And of course I had an answer.

"I can set you up at the Stouffer's in Crystal City, and I can make everyone very comfortable," I told her. "And since we're right next door to National, everyone can be off the plane and relaxing in their rooms in a half hour. I'll make sure of that."

Even the Secret Service liked the idea. The logistics were perfect.

That afternoon I gave Shirley Moore a tour of the hotel, and she loved everything about my suggestion. Stouffer's in Crystal City would provide a much-needed balm for her chafed travelers.

I booked them in, and it was the beginning of a long and fruitful relationship and friendship with Shirley and her staff.

The secret to pleasing guests, I had learned, was doing a little intelligence on who they were and what they liked. I knew from my own trips with the Reagan people that Lyn Nofziger, Reagan's often irascible press advisor, who would go on to serve as Reagan's communications director, was fond of Boodles, a top-shelf British gin that had been Winston Churchill's favorite. Boodles was not the type of liquor Nofziger could easily find at campaign stops in Akron or Peoria, or in most hotel minifridges. When the Reagan people moved to the Crystal City Stouffer's, I made sure a bottle was waiting for him when he checked in.

Soon enough, I had another name to go with Hotel Guy. In some circles I became Judd Boodles. Apparently, I had made a good impression!

Once Reagan and Bush were installed in the Oval Office, I settled back into my job at Stouffer's, content that I had helped, and chalking off my sojourn into politics as a wonderful experience.

It seems the Republican elephant never forgets.

Two years later the Reagan team planned one of the most ambitious summits ever on American soil, the ninth annual G7, set to take place in quaint and quiet Colonial Williamsburg, Virginia, in 1983.

Visiting world leaders would stay in the traditional colonial inns and houses normally reserved for tourists. The G7 would be an onslaught of epic proportions for the normally staid and slow-paced tourist mecca.

Arranging lodging and the flood of details that would accompany the summit while also keeping both the locals and the world leaders and their entourages happy would require an insider's knowledge.

Hotel Guy was back. My life was about to change in a way I would never have imagined.

CHAPTER 8

Williamsburg

I IMAGINE I'D HAVE TO THANK MICHAEL DEAVER FOR THE NEW direction in my career path, though I'm sure I was the last person on his mind when he came up with the idea to hold the G7 Summit, Ronald Reagan presiding, in Colonial Williamsburg, Virginia, in 1983.

Mike Deaver was nothing short of a genius when it came to seeing opportunities for vibrant color where others saw only black and white. Deaver was the creative force behind what would become iconic images that announced to the world—and to American voters—that Reagan was a man of authority, a president who cared. Deaver's talent was such that he picked up a nickname, Magic Mike, for his mysterious ability to choose stunning backdrops for many of Reagan's memorable speeches.

Deaver was behind the dramatic shots of Reagan on the D-Day invasion beaches, backed by the cliffs of Normandy; on the Berlin Wall before it was torn down; on the Great Wall of China; filling sandbags after floods in Louisiana. Deaver directed Ronald Reagan's final shining moment as well—a wide-angle shot of the sun dipping slowly into the Pacific Ocean lapping at the shores of his California ranch after Reagan's moving and nationally televised memorial service in June 2004.

The summit in Williamsburg—a living museum of American history—was one of Deaver's masterworks. Williamsburg had been capital of the Virginia Colony from 1699 to 1780. Modern Colonial Williamsburg is a historic district and living-history museum. Deaver had imagined world leaders convening where American democracy was forged, surrounded by colonial reminders of how America came to be. The pace for the summit would be slow and personal, with the leaders meeting informally every day after more intense negotiations to discuss the matters at hand and the future.

The symbolism was inescapable. The reality was, to put it mildly, challenging. The streets of the historic area are closed to motor vehicles, the surviving buildings restored to their eighteenth-century appearance. Colonial Williamsburg was quaint, and its daily pace was slow and deliberate.

It was possibly the worst place to host what would essentially be a multiday assault of world leaders and the throngs of journalists who would cover them.

How do you fit eight twentieth-century leaders, their support staffs, security people, and the cars and vans carrying them into an eighteenth-century village where motor traffic was forbidden? How do you coordinate the schedules of eight world leaders, find places for them to stay, arrange for them to get to meetings and still have time for the over-the-backyard-fence discussions Deaver had imagined?

Symbolism aside, the G7 would shut the town down for three days and no doubt ruffle a few local feathers. The potential for misunderstanding and embarrassment was huge.

The Reagan team needed someone who could throw the various ingredients into a blender and come up with a smooth and palatable concoction that everyone would savor.

They needed an experienced hotel guy.

My efforts during the campaign had not been forgotten—I got a call.

I enjoyed challenges, and this one was a doozy.

I agreed to step in, this time as a paid staffer. I had enjoyed my work for Stouffer's, but the allure of working for Ronald Reagan and having a hand in this historic summit proved too hard to resist.

Soon enough, I was working under Larry Eastland, a former US Marine who had begun his political career as a staff assistant to Gerald Ford in 1974, then went on to have a very successful business and academic career that continues today.

Deaver had imagined what in effect was an anti-summit, with the leaders staying within walking distance of one another, wrapped in the colonial aura that would serve as a constant reminder of the birth of American democracy. He saw Margaret Thatcher and François Mitterrand chatting casually over a backyard fence, calmed by the pressing influence of the past. Such meetings held the potential for stunning photos and indelible symbolism. The summit would be a uniquely American concoction. It would be, Deaver imagined, an opportunity for world leaders to step back into a rich past to forge a brighter and less contentious future.

The symbolism was rich, of course. But symbolism is an ephemeral concept. My reality would be harsher. Off camera there would be armed and vigilant security teams, a nod to the day's realities. Not seen would be possibly chagrined and puzzled leaders staying in rooms made for eighteenth-century sensibilities and bodies.

My job would be to ease the way. Planning began ten months before the summit.

I was charged with arranging housing for Canadian Prime Minister Pierre Trudeau, French President François Mitterrand, West German Chancellor Helmut Kohl, Italian Prime Minister

Amintore Fanfani, Japanese Prime Minister Yasuhiro Nakasone, and British Prime Minister Margaret Thatcher.

It was a delicate task that required tact, patience, and all the diplomacy I could muster. In a way it was akin to the meticulous planning that went into state dinners, except the principals would be close to one another for days rather than a few hours. Backyard neighborliness went only so far. My team and I had to be very careful.

It would be my first paid assignment in a job that would end years later, as I sat on the steps of the Capitol in Washington, DC, with two of my George W. Bush colleagues, Marlin Fitzwater and John Herrick. George Bush had told us to do everything necessary to accommodate the incoming Clintons.

Hillary Clinton had in turn been gracious to the Bush team, and had at one point asked me if I needed any help. Sitting on the Capitol steps looking down the Washington Mall that afternoon in the brisk January air, Fitzwater turned to me and asked what else we should be doing.

"It's time to go, Marlin," I said. "When you're out, you're out."

I was very much in the thick of things as the planning for Williamsburg took shape. I drove down a month ahead of time to negotiate the tsunami of details needed to have everything ready when the leaders arrived. Another part of my charge was to discuss plans with the local police and with town business leaders, who were nervous about the impending invasion.

My first stop was a meeting with the Williamsburg Hotel Association, a staid group of business owners and tourist visionaries who had created and maintained the allure of Colonial Williamsburg. They did not necessarily need the publicity, and they were wary of the attention.

The advance team had already completed the delicate task of assigning hotels for each leader, and all the leaders but Nakasone and Reagan would stay in colonial-era guest homes.

My job was to inform the hotel association what precisely would happen and how much the Reagan administration would be paying for the disruption. To ease the way, I had to look at the summit not through Mike Deaver's creative eyes, but instead through the eyes of the local businessmen, who were not thrilled.

The biggest annoyance for the hotel owners was the fact that Colonial Williamsburg would be shut down. No tourists would be allowed to mingle. Residents of the area would be subject to scores of security checks. Surveillance helicopters would be flying constantly; sharpshooters would be stationed in houses and on newly erected platforms; bullet-resistant shields were placed on house windows, a distinctly non-colonial touch.

The august members of the Williamsburg Hotel Association were less than enthusiastic about the prospects, and my first meeting with them was the most crucial. They had been made an offer they could not refuse, but they did not have to like it. It was on my shoulders to explain that everything would go smoothly and that life would quickly return to its normal pre-summit pace.

I sat with nine grand old Southern gentlemen around a conference table to discuss our plans, and to assure them that all was well. It was in many ways like telling a group of homeowners that the hurricane projected to hit their town would be mild and pass through quickly. By then, I had the house assignments and the dates. I needed only their consent to move ahead with the final touches.

I knew the key to negotiations was to treat them and their concerns with respect and to acknowledge that we had put them in a tough spot, essentially painted them into a corner.

"How are you going to guarantee this will run smoothly?" one asked me.

"You have my word," I replied.

That was all that needed to be said.

I returned to Williamsburg a week before the Memorial Day summit, where I would serve as the point man for any problems that would arise. There were a few minor snags. There always are, but the event from my side of things could not have gone better.

The leaders found their accommodations comfortable. Williamsburg police were on hand and helpful; the locals accepted the disruptions and, in the end, were buoyed by their short time in the spotlight. There were certainly ample opportunities for press photographers to capture colorful photos of various leaders in horse-drawn carriages on their way to the Governor's Mansion for the main discussions.

Mike Deaver had again struck the right chord in his quest for pomp and ceremony.

My contact with leaders was limited, which for me was the best-case scenario. Intense security prevented idle chitchatting, as one might expect.

In addition to foreign security staffs, there were more than 350 Secret Service agents, close to 200 Virginia State Police, members of the local force, as well as the county police and sheriff's office. Crammed into the tiny town was the added presence of several thousand journalists.

Williamsburg was my first real involvement with foreign security teams and our own Secret Service, who, understandably, were wrapped a little tight and low on humor. As my advance work grew over the ensuing years, I would understand why.

Williamsburg was unlike any summit I worked in my time with Ronald Reagan and the Bushes. There was the possibility for chaos, and danger was everywhere. There were far too many things to control for security people, whose strength lay in control. I don't imagine there were any security guys who were overly enthused with Mike Deaver's visions of pageantry.

I did have a chance to chat with Margaret Thatcher, who popped into a pub while we were taking a rare break for a quick bite to eat. Contrary to her reputation as the Iron Lady, she proved to be lighthearted, close to amused. She had no trouble mixing with the patrons, who were delighted.

But Deaver's vision held true. At one point after a meeting, photographers clamored for a chance to capture Trudeau and Kohl walking down Williamsburg's main street, much like normal tourists on a normal day. They paused briefly outside a tavern to speak to a group of singing waiters. It was not a typical summit photo-op.

From a diplomatic and political perspective, the Williamsburg G7 was considered a success. Reagan preferred to use summits for foreign policy initiatives. He had wanted the Williamsburg meeting to reach a deal to allow the United States to station cruise and Pershing missiles in Europe to counter the Soviet Union's own missile buildup. He did.

Even for someone as comfortable as I was with managing details, the sheer volume of things to attend to left some stray problems popping up as if I was playing a game of Whac-a-Mole. Even with ten months to plan, the timetable to accomplish what I needed to do was too compressed.

I had no say in the matter, of course.

My wife, Gail, a New Hampshire native with a fondness for speaking her mind and an aversion for pretense, stepped in to help manage the torrent of details, a few of which I could never have imagined.

She offered to help coordinate logistics—rooms and transportation and meals for opera star Leontyne Price, who was scheduled to perform at the session-ending summit dinner. Price was the first African American soprano to receive international acclaim and had for years been a leading performer with the Metropolitan Opera in New York City. Gail also offered to help coordinate the lodgings and logistics for a group of chefs who would be providing gourmet meals.

Long before the age of "celebrity chefs," the group brought to Williamsburg proved to be a recipe for disaster. They ran Gail ragged, even with her hotel background. They were demanding, petulant, impatient, and seemingly dissatisfied with arrangements at every turn. It was enough to try even Gail's historic New England patience.

Leontyne Price provided a much-needed balm. She was gracious and grateful and accommodating at every turn.

The difference in attitudes offered an interesting twist on celebrity behavior. An actual diva was anything but, while the chefs were demanding and close to being intolerable, even for Gail.

One could only be grateful they were not at the negotiation table.

CHAPTER 9

Nancy Reagan's Bidet Cloth

I'D BE THE FIRST TO ADMIT THAT DROPPING A ONE-TON DIESEL generator into the courtyard of a palace built for the Spanish royal family more than four hundred years ago was not a good idea.

It wasn't my idea, but as with any presidential trip, the stew of self-interested support groups involved often had conflicting aims. Mine was simple. I was charged with assuring Ronald and Nancy Reagan had a comfortable and uneventful overnight stay in Spain at the gracious El Pardo Palace.

Ronald Reagan was making a state visit to Spain to meet King Juan Carlos I and President Felipe González Márquez in May 1985 and would stay at the gracious El Pardo Palace, which had served as the official residence of dictator Francisco Franco from the end of the Spanish Civil War in 1940 until his death in 1975.

The last American president to visit Spain and meet the generalissimo had been Gerald Ford, shortly before the controversial Franco died and Spanish politics took on a new life. Franco had ruled Spain with an iron hand, acquiring the titles of leader of the nation, head of the armed forces, chief of state, and head of the only legal political party—Spanish legality being another of Franco's powers.

Franco had been a neutral ally of Hitler and Mussolini during World War II and at one point a pariah to most of the world. By the time of Gerald Ford's visit, he had transformed himself into an ally of many Western democracies. In Spain, though, his dictatorship was unpopular.

Democracy was restored after Franco's death, and Felipe González Márquez, a lawyer and secretary-general of the Spanish Socialist Worker's Party, would serve as prime minister from 1982 to 1996.

By the time of Ronald Reagan's visit, Franco's suffocating rule was gone, and a visit by an American president would add a much-needed imprimatur to the nascent democracy, to say nothing about stability to American interests in Europe. Reagan's main purpose was to smooth rough edges and bring the United States and the new Spain into the same orbit.

On my flight from Dulles to Madrid, admittedly naïve, I saw my job as relatively simple, and I had prepared for weeks. I was charged with assuring the Reagans stay at El Pardo Palace was seamless and uneventful, especially for Nancy Reagan, who would relax there while Ronald Reagan was meeting the king and prime minister.

In Washington before the trip, newly baptized in the complicated world of advance work, I was confident the plans I had laid out would fall neatly into place. When I returned home after the trip, I realized the president's challenge was far easier. He had only to begin the process of healing decades of ill feeling and animosity brought on by Franco's autocratic rule and ill-conceived alliances.

I had to deal with the generator, an imperious keeper of Franco's flame named Madame Semprún, and a near-Shakespearian intrusion of political intrigue. The cacophonous generator was far from my only headache. The trip to Spain was my brutal introduction to the infighting and petty territorialism that can arise when too many self-interested aides converge.

On the face of it, it should have been a simple trip. The El Pardo, once used as a hunting lodge for Spanish monarchs, sat on a nearly forty-thousand-acre estate. The cream-colored main building was magnificent, surrounded by tranquil and well-kept parks and forests, with occasional deer wandering the grounds. A grand entrance hall opened to more than thirty rooms, each in its own way kept meticulously by Madame Semprún as an homage to its former resident, Franco.

I would very quickly butt heads with the fastidious Madame Semprún, the self-appointed keeper of Franco's flame, who, while polite, saw the Reagans' overnight visit not as a historic first but as an imposition.

I arrived in Spain six days before the visit to sort out the arrangements. I took a room at a hotel in Madrid and made the forty-minute drive to the palace early the next morning to meet with representatives from the American embassy to gauge the challenges and arrange for solutions. I quickly learned there was much to do.

A presidential visit demands modern communications and airtight security. Reagan needed immediate access to Washington. The palace offered thirty gold-plated telephones that had likely been installed shortly after Franco commandeered the palace forty years before. The antiquated electrical system was connected to porcelain fuses that would blow easily with little more than the draw of a hair dryer. It was a miracle the lights stayed on at all. The power-hungry modern communications systems we brought along to keep Reagan in touch with the rest of the world needed far more than the palace's electrical system offered.

Part of my effort coordinating the Reagans' arrival was to work with a representative from the White House Communications Agency (WHCA). He told me the gold-plated phones would have to go. I had made it a rule not to interfere with the WHCA people or the Secret Service, especially when they were doing their sweeps for possible wiretaps. It was their business, not mine.

An irritated Madame Semprún pulled me aside. She was upset, not at the WHCA representative or Secret Service, but at me. In short order I had become the sacrificial anode for the entire operation, the one man who took the heat generated by everyone else.

I suppose it was her easier path.

Earlier that first day she had again stormed into my temporary office, holding a gold-plated phone that had been disconnected during the security sweep, during which much of Franco's antique furniture had also been pushed to the side.

"How dare you remove these phones," she screamed. "They're antiques."

That was a minor setback compared with the generator. I was unaware of plans for the generator, which was brought in by the White House communications office.

I spent close to fourteen hours at the palace my first day, tending to other matters and trying my best to accommodate the imperious Madame Semprún, who watched my every move. My day culminated with the installation of the World War II military-issue generator brought in on the bed of a rumbling US Army truck without warning. The olive-green monster, complete with a US Army star, took up half the truck bed. Sitting idle in a courtyard outside the fifteenth-century palace, it seemed to me an incongruous addition.

I did not dispute that we needed it, but I felt blindsided by its sudden intrusion. With a little warning, I could have eased the rough seas that were developing between me and Madame Semprún.

I began to detect the slight scent of rebellion in the air.

My time in the army had exposed me to players who had elevated the act of self-preservation to an artform. Never admit a mistake, never call attention to yourself or your actions, and, when in doubt, blame someone else.

That was the army; I did not think such things would be possible in my new line of work.

I'd soon figure out that my embassy counterparts were not interested in helping. I sensed a slight distaste among those career diplomats for Ronald Reagan and his policies. I realized the embassy guys were not about to do me any favors. I'd learn later that they were loath to make any of the necessary upgrades needed to accommodate the president, deciding—for God knows what reason—to side with Madame Semprún, who wanted the sanctity of her beloved Generalissimo preserved.

By the end of my first day, I knew I was swimming against a strong current let loose by not only Madame Semprún but also my own supposed allies from the embassy. The eddies were numerous.

The pièce de résistance of this brewing disharmony came when technicians fired up the generator for a test. I was sitting in my temporary palace office when I felt what seemed to be a small earthquake. The entire palace shook, table lamps vibrated off their perches to the floor, windows rattled. The cacophony deafened me.

Madame Semprún was not pleased, and I became the focus of her wrath. She bolted into my office as I sat there, open-mouthed.

"What are you doing?" she screamed, her face scarlet, pointing out the window to the generator in the courtyard. "This is Spain, not an American military base."

If she could have killed me then, she would have.

To add to my embarrassment, the head of the embassy team followed her into my office, adding his own critique: "This will ruin our relationship with Spain."

I knew then that all my diplomacy and all my patience in dealing with both the embassy crew and Madame Semprún, like the lamps, had just vibrated off the table.

In any situation where territoriality and power—or access to it—are up for grabs, I learned quickly that I needed allies. With three of the four embassy aides trying to sabotage my arrangements, I found one potential ally.

The fourth aide, who happened to work for the CIA, though he was listed as a commercial attaché, pulled me aside and let me know what was going on. My messages and directives were not passed along to their intended recipients. Even the simplest of tasks I had requested were ignored. It was difficult for me to realize that things were going awry. It was a subtle campaign orchestrated by men who were very good at subtlety. The cumulative effect was that things were not going as smoothly as I had hoped.

The Reagans were set to arrive the next day, and the El Pardo Palace was a beehive of intrigue, reminding me of how life probably went on day to day at Versailles those many years ago.

My last unpleasant surprise awaited me the next day, after the Reagans had arrived at El Pardo. The president left in the morning, making the motorcade drive into Madrid for his meetings.

Nancy stayed to relax.

A president's wife is sheltered as much as possible from any intrusions, as it should be. There is a strict protocol for dealing with any situation, and Nancy Reagan valued those protections. Nancy Reagan was inclined to a royal posture. She was not the gregarious sort, not given to informality or chatting amiably to those she viewed as staff underlings. Only her personal aide had access to her. Anything she wanted done would be addressed by her personal aide, and only her personal aide. Those were the rules, and anyone who broke them would be subject to her ample supply of wrath.

I knew from the outset of my new career that I was not to deal with Nancy directly, ever. I was fine with that, needless to say. I made it a point to not go near Nancy Reagan.

With the president in Madrid and Nancy enjoying the comforts of El Pardo, I had breathed a mistaken sigh of relief. A problem was brewing, and I was soon pulled into it.

Nancy's personal aide had gone into Madrid with the president, leaving a vacuum in the chain of command set up to deal with Nancy problems.

As I was sitting quietly in my temporary El Pardo office, a White House steward approached me. "Mrs. Reagan would like to see you immediately."

I walked quickly through those ancient hallways, climbed two flights of stairs, and knocked on her door. She beckoned me inside, where she was sitting on a couch holding a small white cloth.

She held it up.

"Young man, are you in charge of advance?"

"I am, Mrs. Reagan."

"Do you expect me to put this on my face?"

I had traveled enough to recognize that the cloth was a bidet towel, the final tool of the uniquely un-American bathroom fixture that served as a commode, in which participants clean themselves with a spray of water rather than toilet paper.

"I need a washcloth now. Fix it," she demanded firmly.

That was the extent of our conversation.

I was blindsided again, this time by the steward who had approached me in my office. The washcloth was his responsibility, but he was obviously disinclined to own up to it.

I quickly called the wife of the American ambassador and informed her of the dilemma, adding unnecessarily that the situation needed to be rectified immediately.

"I'll bring some clean face towels right over," she said, "and take them directly to Mrs. Reagan."

"No, ma'am," I said. "I will send someone to collect them."

Allowing the ambassador's wife to intrude on Nancy Reagan would have been my final act; she would have fired me on the spot.

When Nancy's personal aide returned from Madrid, I told him what happened; the steward was soundly chewed out.

So much for smooth and uneventful.

I would learn later that Madame Semprún had a tea party the night the Reagans departed and gave bottles of cologne to those she had viewed as helpful. Not surprisingly, I was not invited.

Despite the many Spanish clamors, back in Washington I realized that I had grown fond of my new work. I enjoyed being in the mix with the president and world leaders and having a hand in helping accommodate in my small way what were vastly important meetings.

I valued boundaries and understood my place in the hierarchy. That did not mean I was deferential to those who disrespected my own boundaries and literally went out of their way to make me look bad.

I was, to put it mildly, steamed.

As part of the post-trip review, I informed the deputy chief of mission, second in command of the American embassy, of what his aides had done to throw the trip off-kilter. He was not pleased and told the leader of the crew to apologize to me. He did and, apparently chagrined, offered me his bottle of Madame Semprún's gift cologne.

I accepted his apology but declined the cologne. "You and I are unlikely to ever see each other again," I told him. "And from my perspective, that is a good thing."

Back at home after the trip and its agitations, I also realized that I needed to be involved in everything that happened on my watch. On later trips, no one would do anything without my knowledge. It was a tough lesson in advance work.

On later trips, no one from any agency did anything without my knowing about it.

CHAPTER 10

The Pope's Dais

GOD KNOWS WHAT THE SURVEY TEAM WAS THINKING, BUT BY THE time I got the last-minute emergency call to head to Detroit, it was clear that details were not among the things they had paid attention to.

Take a good dose of haphazard planning, throw in a star-struck Secret Service agent and his parents and an oblivious advance team member who ignored protocol, and add a dash of political tone deafness. I was facing an ominous brew.

My trip to Detroit for Vice President George H. W. Bush's meeting with Pope John Paul II on September 19, 1987, was a recipe for disaster.

Maybe the survey team was overwhelmed by the thought of the pope in America and the adoring throngs of Polish Americans in the densely Catholic Detroit area who were enthralled by the chance to see their hero and attend Mass at the only venue that could accommodate them, the Pontiac Superdome.

Maybe it was simply bad timing. Or perhaps it was sparked because George H. W. Bush had an emotional and compelling reason to meet Pope John Paul II and the survey team was ordered to make the trip perfect. Whatever the reason, the essential details, the minutia so necessary to a smooth visit, were somehow lost in translation.

By the time I got to Detroit, the damage was done, and I stepped into the worst advance trip I was ever involved in. There was nothing I could do to reel it back in and start over. I could only repair things as much as they could be repaired and hope for the best.

At first, shortly after his arrival in Detroit, George H. W. Bush was beyond annoyed, a feat very difficult to achieve for the usually unflappable vice president. He had good reason. Luckily, he calmed down, regained his predictable equanimity, and rolled with the punches. The pope, as always surrounded and insulated, had no idea of the clamor.

We were fortunate and avoided a total debacle; but for a few agonizing hours, that did not seem possible.

By the time I left Detroit, I was relieved and grateful. Most important, I was still employed. At the height of the trip, as I scrambled to repair the damage, I wasn't so sure. Heads would roll after that trip, but mine stayed connected to my shoulders.

I'm not making excuses, mind you, but I would have done things differently. First, by maybe not upsetting a centuries-old papal tradition; second, by not treating a potential photo opportunity with the pope as though he was some sort of Hollywood celebrity. The latter incident, devised by an overzealous Secret Service agent and an advance team aide, was akin to asking the pope to cram inside one of those Woolworth's photo booths popular in the 1970s as it flashed away, four photos for a dollar.

But that's just me, and my respect for a world leader such as the pope and others whose staff I worked with.

It simply wasn't done.

To pour more gasoline on the growing fire, George H. W. Bush's meeting with the pope held special significance. In Washington, we were told that nothing was to interfere with George and Barbara Bush's private meeting with Pope John Paul.

The vice president's thirty-three-year-old son Marvin was seriously ill. He had been diagnosed with ulcerative colitis and had lost thirty pounds. He would eventually be admitted to Georgetown University Hospital to have part of his colon surgically removed.

Marvin's illness had deeply concerned his parents. In a later interview, Marvin would note that his parents had "agonized" over his illness and that his father and mother spent hours by his bedside as doctors struggled to diagnose the disease that was slowly killing him.

The Bushes wanted a private meeting and the pope's prayers for Marvin's health. They also wanted Marvin's full-time caretaker, a Catholic woman, to meet her church's leader in a gesture of kindness and appreciation for her efforts. Everyone on the advance team was aware of the special significance of the Detroit visit, and acutely sensitive of having things go as smoothly and as seamlessly as possible.

To add a little accelerant to the growing flames, George H. W. Bush, heir apparent to Ronald Reagan, was running for president. Everything he did was under a media microscope.

The survey team had been under enormous pressure, which, in retrospect, pushed it into a flurry of carelessness the likes of which I had never seen. After that trip, I made sure the mistakes made in Detroit were never repeated on my watch. It was a tough lesson learned.

I was unaware of the lackluster survey work until I stepped into the middle of it.

The trip started off on the wrong foot and continued that way, due in large part to a lack of strict oversight of the crucial details so important to any trip. If a trip is poorly planned, if details are over-looked and contingencies not established, nothing will go right.

The survey team, it was clear, had rushed the job.

I had not been scheduled to supervise the trip and had nothing to do with the survey or the pre-trip report—the sort of details I spent a great deal of time on, drilling my staff to the point of annoyance. I didn't care about my long pre-trip meetings or the complaints from my staff. Precise planning produced positive results.

Two days before the pope was to arrive in Detroit, my boss, John G. Keller, called me. That call was sure to be ominous, like the "Winds of War."

"Congratulations. You're the new tour director," he told me. "Collamore will help."

Tom Collamore was George Bush's deputy chief of staff. That Collamore was joining me should have been a sign that things were awry. Tom Collamore was a pro who had been through the ringer. He had gotten his start in the political game years before, when he was hired as a driver for Connecticut gubernatorial candidate Lew Rome, then leader of the Connecticut State Senate. Rome asked Tom to drive to the airport to pick up a man named George Bush. The rest, as they say, is history.

"Get to Detroit and straighten things out. It's going to hell," Keller told me.

Tom and I both knew we were the sacrificial lambs. If we could not straighten things out, the blame would fall squarely on us. That's how things work.

The game was on. Collamore and I needed to get things under control.

Pope John Paul II's two-day visit to Detroit had been long awaited. The Polish-born pope had chosen Detroit and its nearby heavily Polish American community of Hamtramck to continue his custom of supporting the Poles at home and abroad.

In 1987 it was clear the pope was having a better season than the usual tenants of the Superdome, the hapless Detroit Lions. His Mass there would be attended by more than ninety-three thousand devout Catholics, more than twice the average of that season's attendance for the Lions, who were having a terrible season and would win only four games in that strike-shortened year.

Still, we gave the Holy Father an opportunity to look inept.

The schedule should have been simple, and better planning would have made it so. After the pope's plane, Shepherd One, arrived at Detroit Metropolitan Airport, he would meet Catholic leaders, visit Blessed Sacrament Cathedral and the Ford Auditorium, and make an appearance at the Hart Plaza. Those formalities completed, John Paul would meet George and Barbara Bush. The historic visit would culminate when he said Mass at the Silverdome.

Tom Collamore and I arrived in Detroit knowing we had to deal with one of the most shortsighted advance surveys I had ever seen.

One of the reasons I planned so meticulously was that I knew once a trip heads south, it not only continues in that direction but gains momentum. A small and seemingly inconsequential misstep becomes a series of pratfalls. Nothing can be done to restore grace.

My instincts proved correct.

Route planning is essential, and management of the motorcade in which the VIPs travel is a crucial task that must appear seamless, for both appearance and security. Apparently, no one on the survey team had checked the route George Bush's motorcade was to take from the airport to his hotel. The lead security car, followed by the vice president's limousine and three other support cars, found itself on a narrow street from which there was no outlet as welcoming crowds watched from the curb. It stopped, unable to move ahead, as Secret Service agents stepped from their car and conferred about what to do next. Finally, the trailing car backed out, followed by the others.

The entire procession then had to re-form as bemused spectators watched, puzzled.

It was a major embarrassment George Bush did not need.

In preparation for the Silverdome Mass, and no doubt with an eye on the political capital George Bush might gain by the imagery, someone—I do not know who and do not, even today, care to learn—convinced the Diocese of Detroit to paint the small dais on which the pope would stand vice presidential blue.

For political imagery, the blue dais made sense, but from any other perspective, it was a horrible instinct.

In their enthusiasm, the survey team had overlooked an important factor. The throngs at the Silverdome were not attending a political rally. They were there because they wanted to be in the presence of the Holy Father, a blessing many would be sure to remember for the rest of their lives.

There was also the small matter of a papal tradition that had been in place since the late 1500s, when Pope Pius V first appeared wearing the white vestments of his Dominican order. White, signifying the peace of doves, had been the symbolic papal color ever since.

Vice presidential blue was not in order.

George Bush, still reeling from the debacle with the motorcade, hit the roof when he heard about the blue dais and called Collamore to his hotel suite. Not being privy to the conversation, I do not know what was said, but I can imagine there was little levity.

Collamore and Bush worked well together, and each man respected the other, but I am certain there were few pleasantries exchanged.

Ever-attentive political reporters and commentators would be certain to notice the jarring blue papal dais. George Bush would have been, pertinent to the principals involved, crucified for putting politics above such a sanctified occasion.

I was thankful after we ordered the dais repainted white that it was relatively small. We were able to have the job done quickly, though I said a silent prayer that the paint would be dry before the pope's Mass.

Both Collamore and I knew the advance team had broken Rule Number One in advance work: "Be Seen and Not Heard," the corollary of which was "Do Your Job and Disappear."

We were in the bright lights. We did not have a chance to pat ourselves on the back, however. More bad news arrived in short order.

Earlier that day, a Secret Service agent had asked the pope's aides to set up a photo opportunity of Pope John Paul with the agent and his parents, a gross violation of protocol. If that weren't enough, a member of the advance team, thinking it was a good idea, asked if he and his parents could join in as well.

The pope's people were apoplectic. Such an intrusion had never been requested.

Fortunately, Collamore and I heard about it before the intruding Americans imposed their will. We apologized profusely and canceled the request. I would be surprised if either the Secret Service agent or the advance aide ever worked a high-level trip again.

I did not sleep the entire time I was in Detroit. Weeks later, I'd still be jolted awake by thoughts of what could have happened if we had not been able to stem the bleeding.

George and Barbara Bush met with the pope, the Silverdome Mass was heralded as a glorious and historic moment, and the vice president's motorcade made it back to the airport without stopping.

Collamore and I had dodged the bullet.

CHAPTER 11

The State of the Unions

OVER THE YEARS OF MY ADVANCE CAREER, I FREQUENTLY FOUND myself in what many might describe as untenable positions. I always figured it out, and always walked away in one piece.

I dealt with angry Russians in Moscow. I had to predict the next move of the unpredictable and lunatic Sendero Luminoso (Shining Path) in Lima. I was forced to calm my mortified French counterpart when we arrived at a summit near Geneva with the force of the D-Day invasion. In Genoa, I diluted as much as I could the testosterone battle raging between Navy SEALs and the Secret Service.

I nearly came to blows with a Nixon acolyte who felt personally bound to defend his former boss against outside intrusions—namely, me.

But the closest I've ever felt I was about to meet my Maker took place in Elizabeth, New Jersey, at what appeared on the surface to be a simple 1984 pollical rally for Vice President George H. W. Bush during Ronald Reagan's reelection campaign against my old boss, Walter Mondale.

That can happen when you offend the Teamsters, a powerful union of some 1.7 million members with a way of influencing outcomes in their favor that was not known for tact or diplomacy.

It began with a simple plan, as these things often begin.

The Elizabeth and Newark waterfront, across New York Harbor from the towering Manhattan skyline, was the perfect setting for the International Brotherhood of Teamsters to become the first labor union to endorse the Reagan-Bush ticket in 1984. It was a big deal, and Teamster leaders had planned to greet George Bush with a line of some one hundred honking tractor-trailers, lights flashing, as he stepped off a tugboat from Manhattan. Union support for Republican candidates, unheard of before Reagan's first win in 1980, was a phenomenon that had given rise to the term "Reagan Democrats."

The shift, with longtime and hard-core Democrats swearing allegiance to Reagan, began when Northern voters, in large part White union members, turned out in favor of Reagan in his victory over incumbent Jimmy Carter.

George H. W. Bush's honking, flashing, and enthusiastic greeting from the Teamsters in Elizabeth on October 12, 1984, would serve to announce that once again, as incongruous as many head-scratching Democrats found it, Reagan would have union support again.

The event was perhaps even more important for the Teamsters, who were often the subject of negative press coverage because of their alleged ties to organized crime. The gala greeting in Elizabeth would allow them to bask in the gentle limelight of a presidential endorsement—to sit for at least a day in the reflected glow and nationwide media coverage of Ronald Reagan and George H. W. Bush.

The Teamsters wanted very badly for the plan to come off without a hitch. Photos and coast-to-coast news coverage of the event would be a godsend for them, and I knew as soon as my boss, John Keller, told me about it that the Elizabeth job was mine. As with every assignment I ever got from John Keller, it came with the tacit warning: Don't screw it up.

Hovering in the background—like the proverbial elephant in the room—of every discussion I would have with union leaders in the days leading up to the event was a fairly steady stream of negative media coverage over Teamster activity and alleged organized crime ties. On slow news days, one could predict yet another story about the mysterious disappearance of former Teamster president Jimmy Hoffa from a Detroit restaurant. One could bet on it. And how such coverage angered union members.

The Teamsters' endorsement of Reagan did create controversy within the labor movement in 1984, and would be a source of tension I knew I had to deal with.

The Teamsters' 1980 Reagan endorsement—an unheard-of change in political order and protocol—had created a lot of hard feelings with other unions. In 1984 the AFL-CIO had expressed hope that the Teamsters would once again return to the fold and back Mondale. The fact that the Teamsters were not going to back Mondale, coupled with their plans to emphasize their Reagan-Bush endorsement with honking and flashing tractor-trailers, did not help me.

In fact, it made my job in Elizabeth tougher, especially since the Teamsters planned to bring a long line of semis into the harbor territory of the International Longshoremen's Association, which were very protective of their territory. There was little love lost between the two groups, and both groups were not above breaking a head or two to make a point if needed. I did not want to get caught in the middle. I did not want George H. W. Bush to get caught in the middle either.

I was only hours into developing a plan when I realized the job would be—to say the least—complicated.

On paper, I had only to coordinate the event, but calming the real-life union tensions was very much a part of my charge. The plan called for George H. W. Bush to arrive in Elizabeth by tugboat. After the requisite speeches, he would depart Elizabeth to a raucous and ebullient Teamsters send-off as he was driven, triumphant, from the harbor front.

For me—event coordinator, organizer, ambassador of goodwill, and the face for the day in New Jersey of the Reagan-Bush campaign—the potential for a down-and-out donnybrook between the Teamsters and the Longshoremen added a bit of pressure. Thanks to a few discussions beforehand, that did not happen.

As it turned out, I would rather have had a fight on the dock. After what did happen, I think I would rather have had my head placed in a vise and asked Teamster President Jackie Presser to turn the handle.

And I believe at one point shortly before the event, he would have done so gladly.

Presser had announced the Teamsters' support for Reagan enthusiastically.

"It is with great, great, great pride that this international organization acknowledges the fact that our membership had an opportunity to vote and cast their ballots for whom they felt would be best to serve this nation," he said.

Presser had come along with his own problems. Earlier that year he had been indicted on charges that included fraud and labor racketeering—only to have the charges dropped when it became known that for years he had been acting as an FBI informant on organized crime.

In the days before the event, I knew my work was cut out for me. With one hand I needed to placate the unions and make sure there were no internecine labor squabbles on the dock so that the

Elizabeth gala went off smoothly. With the other I needed to make sure the Teamsters were happy.

In fact, I met first with the Longshoremen, picked up from my Manhattan hotel and driven by limousine to a small but incredible Italian restaurant in Newark. There I dined with, among others, Thomas Gleason, president of the International Longshoremen's Association, who I had known earlier. We enjoyed a great dinner and had some productive talks about the Bush event.

The Longshoremen would not be a problem.

Once that was scratched off my to-do list, I met two nights later in Washington, DC, with a leadership group from the Teamsters whose job it was to assure that the events in Elizabeth went off smoothly. I knew as soon as I saw them that they were accustomed to getting their way. We dined at the prestigious Palm Restaurant on 19th Street in Northwest Washington. Washington is a celebrity town, and The Palm is a celebrity spot, known for hanging caricatures of famous patrons on its walls for diners to see.

As I sat at The Palm that evening to sew up the final details of the Elizabeth event with my new Teamster friends, I noticed that a caricature of Jackie Presser was looking down on us. I got it. I understood the importance of the dinner we were about to have.

After the dinners in Newark and at The Palm, still in respectful awe of my new companions, I silently connected the Elizabeth-Newark harbor setting to the Marlon Brando movie *On the Waterfront*. Everyone I had met at those dinners was, if nothing else, very cinematic looking—in a way, organized crime caricatures of their own, right out of central casting. If the situation were not very real, I would have dismissed those guys as perhaps overacting B-film extras.

I chose not to point out the similarity to them.

Keller had put me in charge of the occasion because I had become known on the campaign, for better or worse, as the "union guy"—much in the same way I had joined the campaign and advance work because I became known as the "hotel guy."

During my years in the hotel business, I had dealt with top labor leaders during summer convention times, when huge numbers of rank-and-file workers would need hotel rooms and assistance.

I saw these groups as a vital source of income during what were called in the industry "shoulder season," the dog days of summer, when occupancy in big-city hotels was low. These union guys were not resort types, and I would find great rates that would allow them to bring their families for an enjoyable big-city week during the convention.

Those convention days allowed me to meet Presser, a tough character from Cleveland who at one point was actually a truck driver. Those days also allowed me to get to know Shannon Wall, the president of the International Maritime Union, and Thomas Gleason, the president of the International Longshoremen's Association—all of which solidified my "union guy" qualifications, I suppose, for the Reagan and Bush advance people.

Jackie Presser and I had hit it off during our various convention negotiations over the years. I knew he trusted me to make sure the Elizabeth festivities and the tractor-trailer fanfare send-off would be flawless.

For the Teamsters, the plan was pure gold. A line of big rigs flashing and honking for George Bush would create an indelible and hugely positive image for a group that was in sore need of better public relations. For Reagan and Bush, of course, it would have been a massive statement. A longtime group of traditional Democrats backing Republicans?

It would be a great shot in the arm for everyone.

All I needed to do was keep the peace for maybe a little more than an hour, to let George Bush step off the tugboat, say a few words, and depart as the Teamsters and their tractor-trailers saluted far enough from the actual harbor not to offend the Longshoremen.

I would meet Jackie Presser's top aide at the elaborate and delicious dinner at The Palm. If anything, the Teamsters knew how to eat, and the girths of quite a few of them showed it. As we began to tie up the final details for the salute to Bush, I had no doubt Presser's aide spoke for him. The eight other teamster organizers at the dinner listened with rapt attention to everything he said.

To my right was an enormous man, close, I would estimate, to six feet, six inches tall and easily more than 350 pounds. He had an equally enormous appetite. Before a waiter brought menus, my hulking dinner mate called one over and asked for the restaurant's biggest lobster. I assumed he wanted an early appetizer.

"Make sure you butcher it," he told the waiter.

The waiter returned with a monster of a lobster, easily more than ten pounds. It had been suitably chopped up to allow my friend to attack immediately, which he did.

The man to my left told me that Lobster Man had once been shot in the chest during a dispute at another restaurant, pulled himself off the floor, sat back at the table, and continued to eat. Glancing over at Lobster Man finishing his huge appetizer, I believed the story.

After dinner plates had been cleared and we were enjoying brandy and the requisite expensive cigars to cap off the meal, Jackie Presser's aide looked over the assembled group, presumably thinking about potential trouble with the Longshoremen.

"Make sure Judd Swift is protected," he told them solemnly.

I was comforted by that.

I did not realize that, very soon, I would need protection from the very group that had just agreed to provide it.

That sudden change in the tenor of our amicable relationship was prompted the next evening by my advance colleague Bruce Zanca, who had been doing the pre-event survey. Zanca's responsibilities included obtaining Secret Service approval for the long line of flashing and honking trucks.

The Secret Service told Zanca that the arrangement, so important to the Teamsters and so crucial to my own plans to make sure the event ran smoothly, was a security risk. There was no way they would allow it. No matter how much influence the Teamsters might have had on that waterfront, they could not overrule the Secret Service.

The Teamsters would be permitted to line up only the cabs of the big rigs. The trailers had to go because the sheer volume of space they would take up would be too difficult to monitor and protect for the Secret Service. There would be too many places for potential assailants to hide.

Zanca told the Teamsters the evening before the event. I was not there, but I imagine that telling the Teamsters to pull the trailers away was comparable to asking them if they would please sit down and be quiet while they were castrated. Cabs without the trailers would look impotent.

Zanca's proclamation was not well received.

Everything the Teamsters and I had agreed to, everything I had tried to coordinate, evaporated in an instant. And there was only one person the angry Teamsters turned to express their discomfort. Me.

Presser's aide called me immediately and demanded to speak to me as early as possible the next morning, the day of the event.

I knew our meeting would not be pleasant, and I did not sleep well, waking occasionally to pray that my new Teamster friends would calm down, perhaps see reason and welcome the fact that the Secret Service was only doing its best to protect George H. W. Bush.

The thought was laughable.

We met in the parking lot of our hotel just a block from the Elizabeth harbor front. Presser's aide saw me in the dim light of dawn and started in, bellowing like a wounded buffalo.

His screed was accompanied by jabbing fingers and spittle spewing from his mouth. I was subject to what was perhaps the most creative, unique, and near-poetic stream of uninterrupted obscenities I had ever heard, all directed specifically against me and the Secret Service.

His diatribe featured a colorful mélange of common vulgarities used as nouns, adjectives, adverbs, and compound adjectival phrases. I believe he even managed a few subordinate clauses. I'd been in the army but had never heard such parsing.

I did have to admit he had a point. It was a gymnastic verbal effort to be admired, though being the object of the threats did give me pause.

I noticed Lobster Man in the background and calculated how long it would take for him to reach me, given his bulk. Then I questioned whether advance work was really something I wanted to continue.

The diatribe ended just as suddenly as it began. Apparently, Presser's aide needed to release his genuine anger and show his men that Teamsters did not back down from insults, perceived or real—even from the US Secret Service.

October 12, 1984, the big day I had gone through so much for, began as planned.

George H. W. Bush arrived on his tug and stepped off into the harbor-front throng alongside International Longshoremen's Association President Thomas Gleason and International Maritime Union leader Shannon Wall. The unrest I had feared between labor unions had apparently been put aside for the day.

The evening before, in Manhattan, George Bush had debated Democratic vice presidential candidate Geraldine Ferraro, an event that had received massive media attention across the country. In a rare moment of candor after the debate, Bush had told a reporter that he felt he had "kicked her ass."

For me, tense about the event and my own labor problems, Bush's off-the-cuff remark served as a bit of welcome distraction. Reporters were clamoring for a clarification and trying to get Bush's attention and a remark. No one seemed to notice the trailer-less cabs sitting and waiting for Bush's departure.

The atmosphere as Bush waded into the crowd after he stepped off the tugboat was circus-like. We were in New Jersey, after all. A candidate for a local office had apparently decided to take advantage of the massive press coverage of the event and get some free attention. Her workers had placed her campaign signs everywhere, uninvited and without approval. This intrusion, of course, did not fit the plans of my Teamster dinner companions, who were already seething about having to remove their trailers.

One of the freeloading local candidate's organizers began asking people in the crowd to move so he could take photos of his candidate. This was, as they say in war, a bridge too far.

I noticed one of my Teamster dinner companions walk up behind the freeloading local candidate's staffer and ask him to step away. Camera in hand, the guy turned and said something I did not hear. The Teamster promptly dropped him with a left hook to the jaw. He went down like a sack of concrete, his head bouncing off the asphalt.

I noticed him a few minutes later slowly walking away, head down, camera still in hand. The local candidate's signs were soon gone as well, pulled down silently and out of sight by the same group of Teamsters.

Given the attention George H. W. Bush's "kicking ass" comment had prompted, the campaign manager, Ron Kaufman, met him as he stepped off the tugboat and presented him with a pair of boxing gloves.

It was all in good fun. But as Ron handed them to a smiling Bush, I thought to myself how happy I was not to have had to use the gloves to protect myself from the Teamsters.

After the speeches, George H. W. Bush left the harbor front to a raucous send-off from honking and flashing Teamster cabs. No one in the press mentioned the lack of trailers.

The plans had worked.

I would live to fight another day.

CHAPTER 12

The New Castle Debacle

TWO DAYS BEFORE THE 1984 PRESIDENTIAL ELECTION, DEEP IN the heart of western Pennsylvania, a rabidly pro-union area of disaffected steelworkers and coal miners, I'd see a counterpoint to the enthusiastic, horn-honking support the Reagan-Bush ticket got earlier in Elizabeth, New Jersey.

It scared the bejesus out of me.

It also provided a lesson I would adhere to for the rest of my advance career: Don't make assumptions about the people you are presenting the president to; don't stereotype; and never—ever— make plans on the fly.

I was not worried about my own safety during what appeared to be a melee, but I held my breath for George H. W. Bush's. The audience he had come to New Castle, Pennsylvania, to speak to on November 4 was seething—loud and angry, frustrated by layoffs and factory closures and an economy they felt had left them behind.

If the Reagan-Bush team was not entirely certain that candidate Ronald Reagan was well on his way to an overwhelming victory over Democrat Walter Mondale in his quest for a second term, I would have been extremely worried that the jeering and angry crowd was a sign we had blown the election. If the contest had been closer, if Reagan had not built a huge following over the course of his first term, historians today would still be writing about it—the day an overconfident campaign staff scheduled a stop that changed the course of an election.

As it turned out, with the election imminent and forecast by every imaginable pundit to be the landslide it was, that frightening day in New Castle got little media attention.

That day still reminds me of how overlooking the most basic elements of a campaign stop—or summit meeting, or any appearance by a president—can lead to very serious consequences. Sometimes the most difficult thing to see is the one right before your eyes, blatantly out in the open.

We should have known the coal miners and steelworkers of western Pennsylvania would not welcome the aristocratic, blue-blooded George Bush into their territory with open arms. Bush was not of their tribe, nor was he viewed as a politician who understood the realities of the working man who was struggling at the time in western Pennsylvania—in many cases unemployed and shut out from the closed, rusted factories that were becoming part of the area's landscape.

New Castle, within easy driving distance of the iconic Rust Belt cities of Erie, Cleveland, and Pittsburgh, sits in Lawrence County, which at the time of our visit still had an unemployment rate of 12.3 percent. In 1982 their unemployment rate had been 18 percent when the rest of the country was 10 to 11 percent, and many of the jobs lost had been in the steel industry. Although the average unemployment rate that year was 7.5 percent, New Castle's rate still hovered around 12 percent.

Sending George Bush there was a horrible mistake.

I know who thought of the idea, but I find it pointless now, nearly forty years later, to identify him. He meant well, but I think he was overconfident and buoyed by the enthusiastic trucker salute in Elizabeth provided by Jackie Presser and the Teamsters.

I believe too, and this is part of the reality of politics as well, that he wanted to do a favor for Pennsylvania Senator John Heinz, a popular Republican incumbent, scion of the Heinz ketchup family, who would stand to benefit from an appearance with the vice president.

Whatever the reason, I had to deal with it.

That day provided me with a lesson I still hold near and dear. There are no absolutes in politics. It is a strange game that mutates daily, and those with the temerity to predict results and make ironclad proclamations of who will win and why are rarely correct. It is dangerous to paint an election with a broad brush, to fit certain voting blocs into neat and symmetrical cubbyholes. I view polls with suspicion, frankly, and that day in New Castle reminds me why.

There was no question Ronald Reagan was on a roll with his Reagan Democrats and his endorsements from the Teamsters and other trade unions.

There were Reagan Democrats, to be sure. But they did not live near New Castle. These guys were hard-core, no-compromise union men who would just as soon stand in front of a firing squad than vote for the likes of George H. W. Bush or Ronald Reagan, two candidates who in their view had never put in a hard day's work in their lives.

A Hollywood actor and a millionaire Yale oilman were unlikely to wind down in a Pittsburgh tavern with a few Iron City lagers and a shot or two after a hard day in front of the blast furnaces at the mill. The union guys from Pennsylvania would scoff at the idea of supporting a Reagan-Bush ticket.

The Teamsters' support for the Reagan-Bush ticket was genuine, as were the growing numbers of Reagan Democrats. But the advance planners for the November 4 appearance in New Castle made the mistake of thinking that union support was universal. They did not understand the workers of Rust Belt western Pennsylvania.

Referring to the Teamsters' support for the Reagan-Bush ticket, Jackie Presser himself once told me, "We're not a democracy." Yes, the union voted in favor of supporting Reagan and Bush. But that did not mean everyone did.

That day in New Castle, coming at the end of a frenetic last-minute juggernaut of campaign stops for George H. W. Bush, was meant to highlight the administration's support for the working class, especially in an area that had been hit hard by factory closings and high unemployment. The plan called for us to fly into Youngstown, Ohio, for a quick appearance, then make the eighteen-mile cross-border drive to New Castle, where Bush would present a check for $850,000 to city officials as a stimulus to create jobs.

New Castle, some fifty miles northwest of Pittsburgh, was and still is a blue-collar city in a blue-collar region of a blue-collar state. The factory workers and coal miners of the region did not share Jackie Presser's admiration for the Reagan-Bush ticket. These guys, if called, would have gone to war for Walter Mondale, the progressive Minnesotan who, in retrospect, did not have a ghost of a chance against Reagan.

After I saw and heard the throbbing crush of protesters in New Castle, I thought we might have been in a war. The anger of the crowd was so palpable, the vitriol of the chants so acidic and vulgar, I thought at one point that things were about to get physical. I felt we were on the edge of a riot. The tension was at a point where it needed only a spark, and I am convinced the factory yard where Bush was speaking would have erupted.

Speaking, George Bush did not give them one. He ignored the hooting and stayed calm. It was a remarkable scene, the stoic Bush and that seething crowd. I saw that day in New Castle the famous Bush cool that had saved him during World War II, when he parachuted into the Pacific after his fighter jet was shot down in Japanese territory and he waited, sick and vomiting, for rescue by submarine.

The man was unflappable. He gave his speech calmly and unflinchingly, not missing a beat.

I never spoke with George H. W. Bush about that day, and as far as I know he never asked what the hell had happened, which he had every right to do. No one on the advance team was ever called to task for what was, in every way, a boneheaded plan.

I do know that as he spoke, he was thinking about getting out of there as quickly as possible.

I know *I* was.

In the hectic final days of the campaign, it was difficult to keep track of the last flurry of campaign activities, and doing advance work, at least properly, was impossible. We had to do our best under what I can only describe as harried circumstances.

I got a call from my boss at the time, Dan Sullivan, to head up the New Castle appearance. I had a little more than one day to prepare, which is always an invitation for trouble.

I headed down there immediately and met two other advance team members, who had been there for several hours setting up plans for the event. I can praise them for their enthusiasm and team spirit, but not their attention to detail. If they had been more experienced, more attuned to the vibrations of malcontent in the area that were easily read if someone was paying attention, the entire frightful day could have been avoided.

If I had had a chance to spend three days there, I would have strenuously suggested we cancel it.

One day was not enough time to prepare, even under the best of circumstances. There is simply not enough time to sell or give out the tickets that assure we can fill the venue with supporters. It was not enough time to set up the fencing that gave us a way to control access.

Dan Sullivan was throwing me under the bus and hoping I could find a way to make it work. He knew he was sending me into advance hell. He also knew that I knew he was.

It did not matter.

"I will do my duty," I told him.

My first stop in New Castle after checking in with the omnipresent Secret Service was a meeting with mayor Dale Yoho, who could not have been nicer, more cooperative, or more enthusiastic. A vice presidential visit would be a shot in the arm for his city, and he wanted to make the best of it.

Unfortunately, he did not have a clue of the magnitude of details that come with a vice presidential visit.

Yoho took me out to the site of the speech—an old abandoned hulk of a former manufacturing plant, rusted out and dilapidated.

My heart sank. It was no place for photos, nor for anything that would promote favorable press coverage of the event. There was no time to change the venue. There was very little time to set up a sound and lighting system to give George H. W. Bush at least a fighting chance to appear optimistic.

Bush would be speaking from a place of such grimness that even Santa Claus would have been unable to overcome it.

Still, as is my nature, I looked for some way to make a silk purse from this sow's ear of a site. I felt that if we could get enough supporters around the vice president as he spoke, we might be able to salvage some usable and positive news coverage.

I turned to Mayor Yoho.

"How many tickets have you sold or handed out for this?" I asked him, hoping to hear at least a few thousand.

"Quite a few," he told me. "I'm thinking we can get a least sixty people out there on short notice."

I knew we were about to be slaughtered. The Mondale people would have a field day. George Bush speaking on revitalizing the Rust Belt and the economy in general in front of sixty people would make for a powerful, mocking photo of the administration's impotent economic policies.

I felt the need to quash a growing sense of panic. This was not good.

The basic plan was simple. Speaking from a small stage we set up at the factory, George Bush would present a four- by two-foot blowup of a check for $850,000 to the head of the area's redevelopment authority. Then he would make a short speech on the administration's economic revitalization incentives for the area. With him on the stage would be John Heinz and popular Pennsylvania Congressman Tom Ridge, a Vietnam war hero from Erie.

I met Air Force Two in Youngstown and made the drive with George H. W. Bush to the site in New Castle, checking in by radio as we drove with the Secret Service.

I heard my first sign of what was to come over the radio as we approached, an indefinable but ominous sounding background hum—a worrying rumble that grew more distinct. I could not put my finger on it, and at first I wrote it off as radio static.

It was not.

What I heard became very clear as we pulled up to the site.

There was an unruly mob of some twelve hundred Mondale supporters on hand to greet George H. W. Bush, pressing forward as close to our improvised stage as they could get. The Secret Service were caught off guard. Luckily the crowd stopped at the base of the stage. But they did not quiet down. They were chanting, screaming in some cases, and seemed to grow collectively angrier as Bush stepped from his limousine and walked to the stage.

The air filled with obscenities as Bush looked over the crowd and began to speak. He never wavered, never blinked. He continued speaking as people from the crowd taunted him as F-bombs and other inelegant curses flew.

As is typical at events where the inertia of folly takes control, the advance team member in charge of the blowup of the check— the main reason we were in New Castle at all—had left it on the plane in Youngstown. There was not even a photo op.

When things begin to head south, they will continue to head south.

I was frankly embarrassed, not just for George Bush but for the entire campaign. So much for open political discourse.

To make matters worse, as the onslaught grew and showed no sign of abating, John Heinz and his group discreetly left the stage. They wanted no part of it. Tom Ridge, to his credit, stayed through the speech, as did I, of course.

After, we left as quickly and as discreetly as possible, got in the limousine, and headed back to Youngstown. Bush had another campaign stop in New Jersey that evening.

The *New York Times* covered the incident in New Castle.

"Vice President Bush was booed and heckled continuously today as he came to this economically depressed area to announce the awarding of a Federal development grant.

"The unfavorable response started before Mr. Bush spoke and continued throughout his remarks about the Administration's economic programs. At times, he could not be heard over shouts of 'We want Fritz [Mondale].' Mr. Bush, who smiled throughout much of the heckling, told the audience at the end of his remarks, "Wait until Tuesday.'"

Bush did tell a reporter in New Jersey after the incident that he understood the anger, noting that there were "pockets that had not fully benefited" from the administration's economic recovery— which I found to be a masterful understatement. I also found it interesting to hear that Bush later told a reporter in New Jersey that the hecklers in New Castle were "idiots."

On my way home, I compiled my own list of idiots, most of whom figured prominently in planning and executing possibly the worst advance debacle I had ever been involved in.

We had dodged disaster.

The election and the landslide very soon made that remarkably horrid day moot.

In Washington with the Reagans for a speech, my usual list of things to do in hand.
COURTESY OF THE WHITE HOUSE

Dear Judd — With my Thanks, every good wish & Very Best Regards. Sincerely — Ronald Reagan

On Air Force One with Ronald Reagan, returning to Washington after a short hop to Philadelphia. I enjoyed the short hops.

COURTESY OF THE WHITE HOUSE

To Judd Swift   Happy 45th!
Many Happy Returns, too. With Appreciation -
George Bush

On my birthday. George H. W. Bush never missed an opportunity to thank staff for their work.

COURTESY OF THE WHITE HOUSE

Inside the limousine, I was giving George W. Bush's chief of staff, Andy Card, a quick summit briefing. Control was more of a hope than a reality.

COURTESY OF THE WHITE HOUSE

Changing of the guard. On the steps of the US Capitol on Bill Clinton's inauguration day with John Herrick, left, and Marlin Fitzwater. We decided to stay outside.

COURTESY OF THE WHITE HOUSE

The masterful Lyn Nofziger and I at the White House after Ronald Reagan's 1980 victory.

COURTESY OF THE WHITE HOUSE

Manning the limousine line outside the front entrance to the White House at Bill Clinton's 1992 inauguration. Never a dull moment.

COURTESY OF THE WHITE HOUSE

Sitting with George W. Bush's press secretary, Marlin Fitzwater, on the steps of the Capitol at Bill Clinton's inauguration as he says goodbye to a well-wisher.

COURTESY OF THE WHITE HOUSE

No rest for the weary. Giving a last-minute G7 presentation on Air Force One. I drilled my team continuously.
COURTESY OF THE WHITE HOUSE

With George H. W. Bush's friend David Bates on a trip to Australia. A very long flight, much to my chagrin.
COURTESY OF THE WHITE HOUSE

A suitably attired George H. W. Bush and I on a sunset cruise off Oahu at the
Pacific Islands Summit for Climate Change & Sea Level, 1991.
COURTESY OF THE WHITE HOUSE

Teamsters President Jackie Presser and a friend chat with me at a reception before the very interesting Elizabeth, New Jersey, union greeting for George H. W. Bush in 1984.

COURTESY OF US TEAMSTER STAFF OFFICE

A rare shot of a smiling Nancy Reagan on a visit to campaign headquarters to meet with advance staff in 1984. With Mrs. Reagan, we were best seen and not heard.

COURTESY OF THE WHITE HOUSE

With Ronald Reagan's secretary of transportation, Elizabeth Dole.
COURTESY OF US DEPARTMENT OF TRANSPORTATION

The always gracious Ronald Reagan greets me at the seventy-fifth Alfalfa Dinner at the Capital Hilton, 1988.

COURTESY OF THE WHITE HOUSE

Bush supporters, including me, surprise George H. W. Bush on Air Force Two in 1989. The cake was delicious.

COURTESY OF THE WHITE HOUSE

Bipartisan farewell. Senator Fritz Mondale hosted a goodbye party for me before I left for US Army boot camp and my military police tour of Germany in 1970.

COURTESY OF THE WHITE HOUSE

My German police colleagues at a reception in Bad Aibling, Germany. I learned much about international relations and security that would help my advance career later.

COURTESY OF THE US DEPARTMENT OF THE ARMY

CHAPTER 13

Tailhooked

I HAD DONE ENOUGH SURVEY TRIPS BY THE TIME I PACKED FOR Norfolk to believe George H. W. Bush's speech on the aircraft carrier *America* would be a cakewalk. I normally never think that, given the surprises that almost always pop up during surveys.

A president speaking on defense spending from the deck of a proud and distinguished carrier that had served for decades in conflicts around the globe? No problem.

At first blush, I thought it would be a typical day in the advance world, hard and demanding work, but nothing too difficult or unusual.

It was anything but.

Today, more than thirty years later, I remain grateful I still have the fingernails I was convinced I had left embedded in the padded armrest of the lumbering UPS truck of an airplane taking me and my team to the survey.

An American president rarely has an empty moment—let alone an empty day—on his schedule. A presidential calendar is filled from day one until he flies into the sunset at the end of his term.

George H. W. Bush was a very busy man from his inauguration in 1989 until he wished new president Bill Clinton the best of luck four years later.

The start of George H. W. Bush's term was especially busy, perhaps even daunting, but he knew the ropes and how Washington worked and took his tight schedule in stride. The advance team did the same, planning and sorting out the logistics for three tightly scheduled speeches that would be covered nationally, one after the other.

Bush was sworn in on January 20, 1989, and delivered his first major speech in front of thousands on a chilly and blustery day at the inaugural. He would give his first State of the Union address three weeks later, on February 9. Because the presidential schedule abhors a vacuum, he would give a major speech on defense spending from the deck of the US Navy aircraft carrier *America* on January 30.

The *America* speech was mine.

How hard can that be? I thought.

The occasion would be a blend of symbolism and power in front of an adoring and rabidly supportive audience. The venue, a stage on the deck of the *America*, was perfect. He need not have said a word, frankly, because there was no need for persuasion in front of that crowd. I knew from my time doing advance work for Ronald Reagan—and for Bush as vice president—that symbolism and strong visuals trumped rhetoric every time. Audiences, even some cynics in the media, are usually swayed by settings and by the emotions those settings spark more than the words spoken.

George H. W. Bush, a World War II pilot and hero, speaking on the need for robust defense spending from the deck of the hallowed *America*, a warhorse of a ship that had served for decades in hot spots around the globe, was a rich and fertile opportunity for stunning front-page photos and positive coverage.

I wished I had thought of it.

When my boss, John Keller, informed me of my assignment, I felt I had only to double-check the details, not reinvent the wheel. Even the venue was accommodating, I thought, since the *America*'s homeport, Norfolk Naval Base, was a short hop of a flight from Washington.

George H. W. Bush's inaugural address was well received. He was in a tenuous position as the new president. Having served as vice president under the extremely popular Ronald Reagan, he nonetheless had to address a growing discontent in Congress precipitated by eight years of Reagan's conservative politics. Bush needed to offer an olive branch and the opportunity for Democrats to note that he was open to bipartisan negotiations.

At the time, more than thirty years ago, observers had been concerned about what they saw as a growing rift between the Democrats and Republicans in Congress and among voters. Looking at those days in my 2023 rearview mirror, I can see how that rift has now become a chasm; but George Bush was genuinely worried and sought to mend fences.

"A president is neither prince nor pope," Bush told the inauguration audience and those listening across the country. There would be no imperious leadership from Bush, who had taken some shots for what some voters perceived as his blue-blooded, out-of-touch vision of America. As a longtime Bush supporter, I was not only buoyed to be working for him, but also deeply gratified about the course he was taking.

I felt he was off on a good footing.

That down-to-earth empathy George H. W. Bush had expressed in his famous "thousand points of light" speech was genuine. Anyone who worked with him or for him would tell you that. He was a caring man who made people who worked for him feel appreciated.

I do not believe he ever heard about the lengths the advance team took on our survey trip for his speech on the *America*. If he had, he would at the very least have given us all a good-natured ribbing.

Survey trips, the painstaking and deliberate pre-event inspections of everything a president is about to step into, are never easy. They do, however, have a certain predictability. I would travel to the city, talk to local police and security people about the potential for danger and the steps being taken to avoid it. I'd meet and discuss details with the Secret Service, study planned motorcade routes and the political flavor du jour, especially in foreign countries. I'd check the weather and the activity from those who might be opposed to what the United States was doing—and there always were and are people opposed to what the United States was doing.

A survey was never easy and could take a week or more. Whenever I left for a survey trip, I knew long hours, a torrent of stress, little sleep, and bad food were in store. These trips were neither exotic nor enjoyable, no matter how the destination appeared in tourist brochures. We were not tourists. We were workers.

In a perverse way, though, I loved survey trips because of their challenge. I loved creating the solutions to those challenges and overcoming obstacles. When the main trip is over and the president is heading home to the White House after a good speech or a satisfying and well-covered summit, there is no better feeling.

So of course, charged with surveying for the *America* speech, I was almost overjoyed.

The speech was on an American aircraft carrier docked at one of the largest American navy bases in front of US Navy men and women. And it was in Norfolk, a short hop from Washington.

My God, I thought, *how easy.*

Keller did not fill in the details of what awaited me and my advance crew of twelve. He told me only that I was to take a Marine Corps transport helicopter to Norfolk, a forty-minute flight, and meet with my counterpart, a towering six-foot, five-inch admiral and former navy aviator.

I assumed—and I note here that I should have known better than to assume anything—that after our briefing with the admiral, we would drive to the pier off which the *America* was anchored and take a short, perhaps even pleasant, launch trip out to the august aircraft carrier.

We landed at the base after an uneventful flight in the clear winter air, disembarked, and walked to a nearby Quonset hut where we would meet the admiral, a man I would characterize most accurately as "an old salt." He was certainly a man of few words who, I suspect, had a dark sense of humor and little use for a group he perceived as a bunch of fussy Washington bureaucrats.

Sitting unsuspecting in the Quonset hut, we all watched as the admiral burst in, his arms wrapped around four helmets and life preservers, which he promptly dumped on a conference table. An adjutant behind him carried more of the same.

Then he turned to me.

"You probably don't know this yet, but we're flying you out of here in a half hour," he said.

I looked at him, flabbergasted.

"Why?" I asked.

"The *America* is currently en route to Norfolk and is now about two hundred miles away, off the coast of North Carolina," he replied.

This announcement did nothing to calm my usual agitation with flying. My piece-of-cake assessment of the Norfolk survey trip had just evaporated. I was not a happy man.

We were escorted to a two-engine propeller-driven plane that, as I mentioned earlier, did not look much different from a boxy UPS truck. We boarded, all twelve of us facing aft.

Before takeoff, the pilot, wearing a US Navy flight suit, left the cockpit, climbed down a short set of stairs, and walked over to me.

"Afternoon," he said. "A few quick notes. Weather is good and there should be no problems. Flight will take about an hour," he added.

Then he spoke the words I remember so clearly to this day. They presaged the most frightening flying experience I have ever had. And coming from someone who hates flying, that takes some doing. It was *Guinness World Records* material.

"We're going to be tailhooked when we land."

"What's that?" I asked, innocently.

"Let's just say we will stop abruptly when I land on the carrier deck," the pilot said.

Then he turned, climbed the stairs to the cockpit, stepped inside, and closed the door behind him.

My anxiety level rocketed.

Fifty minutes later, the pilot called me to the cockpit. I unsnapped my seat belt, traversed the short aisle, and climbed up. Below us, set against a startling blue sea and looking the size of a postage stamp, was the *America*.

"We'll be landing in fifteen minutes."

"Oh, my God," I said.

I returned to my seat and buckled up.

We began our descent. I stared at the back of the plane, my fingernails digging into the armrest, the tendons in my forearms stinging. We dropped quickly, although I could see nothing but the rear door of the plane.

When the plane's tailhook caught the *America*'s arresting cable, I felt my teeth drop to my stomach. My brain strained to remain active as the tremendous G-force squeezed every bit of oxygen from my head. I saw brilliant shafts of light and stars. I wondered briefly if I would pass out. In an odd moment of clarity, I recall that I was thankful I had not eaten anything that day.

We stopped, and, to be clear, we did not roll to a stop. We were flying, then we were not. I swore that I would never—ever—let myself be put into such a position again.

The entire survey team, not surprisingly, was a bit disoriented as we stepped gingerly from the plane to the deck of the *America*. But we were professionals, and we quickly pulled it together.

The *America*, commissioned in 1965, had a hallowed history, serving three tours in Vietnam and in numerous crises in the Middle East and Mediterranean. After our visit it would go on to serve in both George H. W. Bush's Operation Desert Shield and his son's Operation Desert Storm.

On deck, the tailhook landing completed and never to be repeated, the survey snapped back into its normal pattern. I was washed in a wonderful normalcy. In fact, I supervised the survey with boyish enthusiasm. The *America* was as close to being hermetically sealed as possible, which was perfect. My original thought—after Keller had informed me of the job and before I learned about the tailhooking—returned. It would be a cakewalk after all. We were surveying an environment we could control totally, which was as rare an occasion as finding unanimous bipartisan support for a bill in Congress.

George Bush would speak from a stage on the *America*'s deck, in front of sailors and officers and a specially selected audience. There were no unknowns in a scenario like that, and it made the survey team's effort all that much easier. The Secret Service crew I worked with agreed. On the *America*, two hundred miles off Norfolk, the usual cretins I looked to neutralize would not blend well with the uniformed crew.

Instead of the foreign officials I dealt with at summit meetings, usually with agendas of their own that did not dovetail neatly—or at all—with what we wanted, I had a crew of enthusiastic US Navy men and women chomping at the bit to help me in every way.

I felt blessed. I breathed easier.

On my walk-through, my normal concerns abating, I was filled with an almost boyish enthusiasm. I was surrounded by the concentrated bustle of F-15s landing and taking off in such close quarters in an elegant and precise ballet as deck crews and pilots worked together. Watching a fighter jet shoot off into the blue Carolina sky above the *America* took my breath away.

Watching, I became a young awestruck boy, imagining himself a fighter pilot about to fly off and save the world.

We completed our survey in six hours, which included a wonderful, lighthearted meal with the captain and top officers, all of whom were accommodating to the extreme and very proud to have been chosen to host the new president in two days.

I nearly forgot that we had to return to Norfolk on the same plane we had arrived on, which had been towed to the side to allow normal flight traffic. I momentarily froze, wondering how the boxy aircraft would ever make it aloft. But I took great comfort from what I had seen of the acrobatic deck crews and how they managed the complex mission of landing jets and sending them off what amounted to a very short runway.

I was calm when we were catapulted into the air smoothly, quickly, and efficiently. I made a silent vow that I would stay clear of aircraft carrier landings or anything that even remotely resembled them for the rest of my life.

So far, that vow has remained unbroken.

George H. W. Bush's defense budget speech went off without a hitch from the deck of the *America* in Norfolk.

CHAPTER 14

Toe-to-Toe with Lech Wałęsa

A CHARISMATIC MAN, LECH WAŁĘSA HAD THE EAR AND COUNSEL of Pope John Paul II, a fellow Pole. Wałęsa's tenacity and fearlessness over the years had earned him the love and respect of much of Poland. Poland's Communist leaders feared him but could do little to stop Wałęsa's growing populist Solidarity movement, which at one point had been banned but not silenced.

An electrician by trade at the Lenin Shipyard in Gdansk, head of its union, and a longtime dissident and political activist, Lech Wałęsa patiently developed enough power and influence to bring the president of the United States to Poland.

In July 1989 President George H. W. Bush made a trip to Poland to meet the mustachioed, no-nonsense firebrand, and I was coordinating the arrangements. By then, Wałęsa had become the darling of the Western press, a man of the people who had shrewdly thrust himself into the final stages of a long and contentious fight to end Communist rule.

In Poland for ten days before the visit, I began to feel as if a vise was slowly closing in on me.

George H. W. Bush had given Poles hope that the outside world was listening during his last visit there in 1987, as vice president. On that visit he had made a televised speech in which he mentioned his excitement at meeting Wałęsa, spoke of the virtues of freedom, and made subtle references to the value of democratic change.

George H. W. Bush was a popular man in Poland. Now he was returning as president, and his visit would no doubt fan the flames the Polish leadership would rather have seen smothered.

There was a lot on the line.

I had met Lech Wałęsa shortly after I arrived, when I was just beginning to set up arrangements. I noticed a spark of the irascibility that had served him well over the years. Our plans had called for George Bush to have a simple lunch with Wałęsa and his wife at their home in Gdansk. I had gone there to assess the arrangements with a team of communications experts who needed to install secure lines and bring in equipment that was out of scale in the small house. The setup process was disruptive, no doubt, but had to be done.

While crews were moving furniture and running lines, I watched as a Volkswagen bus pulled into the driveway. As always through the trip, I had an interpreter at my side. I did not need one to see that the feisty Mr. Wałęsa was very annoyed.

He stepped from his van, yelling. I would learn from my interpreter that Wałęsa had asked me, "What the hell are you doing here? Why are you bothering my wife?"

I'm certain some choicer words were dropped from the translation, but I got the message.

When I met Wałęsa for the second time, George Bush was set to meet him for a daylong series of public events, and there was little time for equivocation. I needed some answers and Wałęsa's help coordinating a very busy day ahead.

Lech Wałęsa had not achieved renown and influence through politeness and charm. He was a hard man and a master of the ways of power. He knew what he wanted and got it. And people loved him.

I sat in front of him in a room at the union hall and explained the schedule for the next day's events and what he was required to do. It should have been a simple exchange. Wałęsa would benefit greatly from the coverage, and the photos and television images of him standing with Bush were certain to be broadcast worldwide.

Wałęsa looked up at me from behind the table where he sat, impatient and seething at what I'm sure he felt was an imposition on his time.

He stared, then slammed his hand down, the sound startling everyone in the room.

I admit being startled as well, but not surprised. That is often how people with power react.

"Why am I dealing with underlings?" he said as he looked directly at me.

During my time in Poland I would face more opposition and interference than any other advance trip I made in my career. I had been prepared for it. The Communist leaders of Poland needed George Bush and the economic influence of the United States, but they were not enthusiastic about it.

By then the writing was on the wall. In an election the month before, Solidarity candidates had won 160 of the 161 seats in the lower house of the Polish parliament and 92 of the 100 seats in its senate. Those races would signal the beginning of the end of Communist rule in Poland.

The timing for George Bush's visit was impeccable.

But Poland in 1989 was an advance man's hell.

I had been assigned a Polish minder who thought I was CIA. I had been followed continuously. I had to be extremely careful about anything I said, knowing it would be reported to the Secret Police.

I had seen thousands of flyers we had distributed announcing President's Bush's visit mysteriously disappear. I would witness a brawl between various Solidarity factions scuffling to gain the greatest advantage at a time when the entire world would be watching.

Despite the agita, helping bring the president of the United States to Poland was one of the most gratifying, soul-restoring trips of my career. Watching the sheer power of people seeking basic human rights and dignity—what we know as freedom—overcome the hard-handed tactics of a police state too long in control was overwhelming. It was political influence in its best and clearest light, free of ulterior motives. Bush was in Poland to influence change, and ultimately he did. The Polish people wanted what Americans had, and George Bush was welcomed like a returning champion.

Over those ten days in Poland, I shared vodka toasts and conversation with the men assigned to sabotage everything I did. I saw children playing baseball in the streets, a game arranged by the American embassy and the US Secret Service, which also supplied the equipment. As the children played, parents enthusiastically cheered, so anxious to take part in something so quintessentially American. I attended Mass, a ritual that many in the overwhelmingly Catholic nation held so dear to their hopes for better lives.

The steady stream of roadblocks did not dilute the electrifying power of democracy at its best.

Still, I had not expected Lech Wałęsa to become a thorn in my side.

After he slammed his hand down on the table in front of me, I knew had to deal with him. I think he was feeling the pressure too.

I stood quickly. Then I slammed my hand on the table.

"Mr. Wałęsa, you need to cooperate if you want to deliver a message to the American people."

I thought he was going to spit. People did not talk to Lech Wałęsa in that manner.

I had a job to do, and I stood my ground. I had had enough interference from the Polish government already. I did not need the star of the show to begin acting like a prima donna.

"We need your help, please," I said, politely but firmly. "There is much to do before you meet President Bush, and you are the only man who can make it happen."

Hoping Wałęsa would respect someone who did not back down, I added, "I'll tell President Bush you are a bully."

That fact that George Bush would never ask me about Wałęsa or, for that matter, speak to me at all, did not enter into the equation. If Wałęsa saw my remark as impertinent, I would be on the way home before Bush landed in Gdansk. I worried briefly I had had crossed the line.

Wałęsa calmed down.

The itinerary we had designed in Washington called for the president and his wife, Barbara, to arrive on Air Force One at Okęcie Airport in Warsaw late in the evening of July 9. The next day he'd lay flowers at the Tomb of the Unknown Soldier, meet with Jewish community leaders, then with General Wojciech Jaruzelski, president of the National Council. Such events are typical, and ceremonial duties are common to many presidential visits. More serious policy talks would follow the next day.

The third day of the visit was powerfully symbolic and emotional. Bush would travel to Gdansk, attend a concert at the Basilica of St. Mary, have breakfast at Wałęsa's home, and travel with Wałęsa to the Monument to the Fallen Shipyard Workers, where Bush would lay a wreath.

I had flown into Warsaw eight days before the Bushes arrived. On paper, it was in many ways a typical trip and typical advance work. However, plans and itineraries typed neatly on paper do not capture the emotion of the actual events.

Bringing a president to a Soviet Bloc country is fraught with security issues, the most prominent being communication. Unsecured calls were sure to be tapped; casual conversations, a simple slip of the tongue, or a throwaway remark would be heard and reported to the Secret Police. No one was who they said they were.

I took the prudent course and assumed that anyone I spoke with had ill intent. It made things much simpler.

My first meeting was at the American embassy with the ambassador and his number-two man, the deputy chief of mission. Ambassador John Roger Davis Jr. was later named by Director of National Intelligence Dan Coats as the fourth person—after Lech Wałęsa, Soviet leader Mikhail Gorbachev, and Pope John Paul II—who had "the most critical role in bringing about the collapse of communism in Eastern Europe."

Davis knew the game. He explained to me, in the embassy's secure, soundproof, untappable SCIF room, the utmost need for caution in any discussions I had, anywhere. I was also told that the Polish government would try to sabotage everything we did. Having things go wrong on any presidential trip is close to inevitable. That's the nature of the advance business. Being told there were people planning to make things go wrong was a new one for me.

I got to work, the first order of which was meeting Major Ribi, my Polish counterpart, who, I was told, would help me with anything I needed. I took that with a grain of salt. I would discern later that my friend Major Ribi had assumed I was with the CIA.

It made for an interesting relationship, since neither of us believed a thing the other said.

At one point, as we settled into our discussions, Major Ribi, who was always accompanied by a group of associates who looked to be no strangers to breaking a head or two if necessary, pulled me aside.

"What are you really doing here? What is your mission?"

He asked me what type of passport I carried.

As a member of the presidential delegation, I had a diplomatic passport, which gave me diplomatic immunity, a get-out-of-jail-free card in a foreign country.

"You're lucky," he said.

My main duties focused on Bush's visit to Gdansk, Wałęsa's hometown and the site of the shipyard where Wałęsa had begun his work as a union organizer. Gdansk would be the high point of the visit.

I visited the shipyard itself with my staff and Major Ribi and his associates to assess the atmosphere. We ended the tour with a boat trip around the works, accompanied by more vodka and beer than I had seen on any deck anywhere.

I was very careful; but for Ribi and his thugs, the alcohol, and plenty of it, was a social lubricant that revealed their true feelings. They wanted photos with us. They wanted to know more about the United States, what life was like, and what freedoms we had. The boat deck became a mini–summit meeting. I returned to the dock thinking that perhaps their hearts were not in their work.

Mind you, that did not stop them from performing it. Thousands of flyers we had distributed announcing George Bush's visit were torn down. Hearing that was disconcerting, but as I spent more time in Gdansk over the next few days, I would realize we did not need flyers. Everyone knew President Bush was coming.

I would see the incredible power of faith, and its usefulness as a political influence, when I met Father Henryk Jankowski, a Roman Catholic priest, Wałęsa confidant, and vocal member of the

Solidarity movement, who used the pulpit at St. Bridget's church in Gdansk to spread the word.

He was singularly responsible for raising the thousands of adoring Poles who lined the streets during President Bush's visit to Gdansk. Later, I would see Jankowski's influence, actually feel it. (Father Jankowski would later become a controversial figure after he was charged with being a pedophile, although he was never convicted.)

President Bush was to attend a concert at the Basilica of St. Mary. I toured the church to view camera angles and seating arrangements with Lynn Kennelly, an advance aide who was a devout Catholic. Father Jankowski gave us a tour, after which he invited us to a Mass over which he would preside.

During his sermon, he introduced us to the assemblage, close to fifteen hundred people packed tightly into the pews.

I stood, embarrassed, but overcome by the emotion. I felt their passion, their desire for freedom, and the hope that had expressed itself in the elections the month before. I knew, standing there in that tightly packed church as people applauded Lynn Kennelly and me, that President George Bush would have a safe and fruitful visit.

I was not wrong.

Bush and Wałęsa were met at each stop in Gdansk by adoring crowds who lined the motorcade's path three and four deep, cheering and throwing a blizzard of flowers so thick on the roadway that drivers had to rely on instinct to know where to go.

George H. W. Bush was welcomed with open arms.

In December 1990 Lech Wałęsa became Poland's first freely elected president in sixty-three years, and the first non-Communist head of state in forty-five years.

CHAPTER 15

"Vitai Lampada" in Bermuda

AN ENGLISHMAN'S GARDEN IS SACRED. THAT IT BELONGED TO THE governor of Bermuda made it especially sacrosanct.

The White House communications office, efficient and focused, took a more irreligious approach to their work—as always, more concerned with efficiency and results than tact—and it nearly did in a summit meeting.

A quintessentially British poem nearly one hundred years old that I conjured from my days in an English school saved the day.

I recited it verbatim to Desmond Langley, an Eton- and Sandhurst-educated major general, in a room full of ancient ceremonial swords he had shown me with great pride over drinks and cigars. I had met Sir Desmond earlier in the day and explained to him the schedule of the one-day summit between George H. W. Bush and Margaret Thatcher on April 13, 1990, and how it would end with a black-tie dinner at his residence, the stately Governor's House.

I had had a taste of the elite British school system years before, as a student at the Rodney School in Kirklington, Nottinghamshire, when I was sixteen. The rigid Rodney School had tested my resolve. There I learned the value of teamwork, lessons I was still applying in my advance work. But I had also been rudely introduced to the darker side of the class-conscious British system, where family ties and birthrights lent themselves more to success than hard work.

Still, I found much to admire about British courage and sense of duty.

The poem "Vitai Lampada" had inspired me and consoled me at a time when I was alone in my Americanness, an outsider at an elite English school where outsiders are unwelcome and my classmates, the sons of British aristocracy, prickly.

The poem had given me purpose.

Written by Henry Newbolt in 1892, a time when the sun truly did not set on the British Empire, "Vitai Lampada" seemed to me to be a darkly beautiful and powerful description of British honor and directness in pursuit of a righteous cause. It speaks to duty and idealism when all is lost.

The narrator's commander has died in battle and he knows he will suffer the same fate. He does not flinch.

My host knew of what I spoke and was taken aback, suddenly silent as I recited.

> *There's a breathless hush in the Close tonight—*
> *Ten to make and the match to win—*
> *A bumping pitch and a blinding light,*
> *An hour to play and the last man in.*
> *And it's not for the sake of a ribboned coat,*
> *Or the selfish hope of a season's fame,*
> *But his Captain's hand on his shoulder smote—*
> *"Play up! play up! and play the game!"*

Major-General Desmond Langley had played the game. Commissioned into the Life Guards in 1949, he had served in Egypt and Libya, and had fought in the Indonesian-Malayan conflict of the 1960s.

He later commanded the London District and supervised the military's participation during the wedding of Prince Charles and Lady Diana Spencer, a duty sure to catch the eyes of the right people. He later served in Cyprus before retiring to become governor and military commander in chief of Bermuda, a British Dependent Territory, in 1990. For Desmond Langley, it was a plum assignment that allowed him to tend to his luxuriant garden, which he had proudly showed my earlier that day.

I continued reciting, an American advance man in Bermuda to make sure George H. W. Bush's meeting with Margaret Thatcher went according to plan.

The sand of the desert is sodden red,—
Red with the wreck of a square that broke;—
The Gatling's jammed and the Colonel dead,
And the regiment blind with dust and smoke.
The river of death has brimmed his banks,
And England's far, and Honour a name,
But the voice of a schoolboy rallies the ranks:
"Play up! play up! and play the game!"

Desmond Langley simply stared, his unspoken question hanging in the air, mixing with the smoke of our cigars.

"I attended Rodney School," I told him, adding that the poem had meant much to me at the time and was etched into my memory.

I had won a friend. I would soon need him.

The White House communications team was about to arrive and do their usual work to assure that George Bush would have immediate access to the world outside the impressive Governor's House, where he would stay. The thirty-room mansion sat on a hill outside the capital of Hamilton. It was surrounded by sprawling lawns on the thirty-three-acre estate, where such notables as John F. Kennedy and Winston Churchill had planted ceremonial trees.

The gardens were expansive and lush, filled with antique cedars, spice trees, and fragile subtropical flowers.

It was, I would soon realize, too inviting a target for the communications guys. If they had annoyed Lech Wałęsa in Gdansk and agitated Madame Semprún at El Pardo Palace, they were about to send Major General Sir Desmond Langley into orbit.

George H. W. Bush and Margaret Thatcher were in Bermuda to discuss the unprecedented events in the Soviet Union, their old archenemy. Mikhail Gorbachev's liberal reforms of perestroika and glasnost had led to populist uprisings in Eastern European countries, long under the Soviet thumb. It was a brave new world, and the old cold warrior Thatcher sought to counsel and caution the newcomer Bush.

On Air Force One heading to Bermuda, Bush had told reporters that Mrs. Thatcher had a "clear view of the world."

I agree, even now, that Margaret Thatcher was the most important and influential British prime minister the United States has ever worked with.

I was an admirer of "The Iron Lady." I liked her politics and her directness. Margaret Thatcher was a strong leader, and I believe she had made an appreciable difference in influencing Ronald Reagan's hard-line policies toward the Soviet Union to become even harder. Theirs was a genuine love affair, bonded by their conservative politics and respect for each other.

I have often thought that Margaret Thatcher's trademark accessory, the heavy purse she carried with her always, was a public relations coup, a subtle image of latent force. Should a recalcitrant politician argue with her, or disagree with her, a metaphorical swing of that purse would make her point. And she made her point often. She could deal with anyone.

At the one-day summit, Bush and Thatcher would focus on the collapse of the Soviet Union and how best to react, but would also touch on the upcoming reunification of East and West Germany and the efforts of Lithuania, Estonia, and Latvia to break from Moscow.

In perhaps an augur of the unpredictable chaos that would soon insert itself on the world stage, later they would also discuss the downing of a Pan Am jetliner over Lockerbie, Scotland, by suspected Libyan terrorists.

It was a powerful agenda set against a backdrop of British pomp and ceremony, which included Bush and Thatcher taking part in a kite-flying contest with schoolchildren during a break from the talks.

Despite the headiness and serious nature of the talks, and my role in making sure everything ran smoothly, that kite-flying contest was a source of some anxiety for me. I had nightmares of George Bush being unable to get his kite airborne as the world media watched.

Bush had, in jest, told reporters before the contest, "I'm one of the better kite flyers. I have a large inventory of kites."

The contest organizer, obviously knowing on which side his bread was buttered, had told the same reporters after the contest, "I wouldn't say he was best. The prime minister did better than him."

It was all in good fun, and the event went off flawlessly.

The summit concluded with a black-tie dinner at the governor's mansion, which I attended in the background, my favorite place.

To prepare for Bush's overnight stay at the mansion, the White House communications guys had taken a direct route through

Desmond Langley's gardens with their thick cables, trampling flowers and dragging equipment through meticulously raked beds.

As we were tending to dinner details, I heard the result before I saw the damage. Desmond Langley was screaming at the crews running the lines. Actually, he was bellowing.

I turned to my assistant, Kevin Moley, a former US Marine who would go on to various high-ranking posts at the State Department, and asked, "What is going on?"

"I'm not sure."

In the distance, outside the mansion, I heard the major-general.

"You bloody buggers. Get out of my garden. How dare you?"

He was not happy.

I went to him immediately, apologized, and promised to make amends. The major-general was not a man easily placated, and if I had been anyone else, he would have continued bellowing and gone right to George Bush.

He saw it was me and calmed, echoes of "Vitai Lampada" still fresh. I'm sure my recitation the night before had saved the day.

Later at the dinner, Desmond Langley told me he was going to make me recite the poem to the entire room.

I begged him not to.

"Please don't do that."

One thing I had learned by then in the advance business is that inserting oneself in the main event, emerging from the background and seeking face time and visibility is not a good idea. I always remembered that I was staff, and staff can be replaced effortlessly and quickly.

Ostentation is a two-edged sword, with the sharpest edge pointed directly at the self-seeker. That was something I drilled into my staff: Be invisible; stay out of the picture—it detracts from the power that surrounds you.

I stayed in the background during the dinner, thankfully silent. There would be no poetry that night.

After the dinner, I passed Margaret Thatcher in a hallway. She seemed to have recognized me from Williamsburg, where I had briefly chatted with her at a pub. One of her strengths as a politician was her ability to speak to anyone. Still, I was surprised she recognized me.

"Oh, hello," she had said with a hint of recognition.

That was the last time I would see her. I was deeply saddened when I read of her death in 2013.

As the summit closed and we were breaking down our operations, I stopped by for a chat with the head of the White House communications team.

"Next time, let me know what you're doing before you do it," I said.

"Of course," he replied.

I doubted it did any good.

CHAPTER 16

George H. W. Bush's Texas Whoop-Up

THE TURF WARS THAT BEGAN WITH MADAME SEMPRÚN IN SPAIN never stopped. They continued in varying degrees through the entire twenty-two years I was on the job. Territorial spats were as predictable as the rising sun. Throughout, I reminded myself more than once of something the poet T. S. Eliot, a favorite of mine, wrote many years before.

We shall not cease from exploration
And the end of all our exploring
Will be to arrive where we started
And know the place for the first time.

Adapted, it fit my job to a tee.

Each presidential trip brought its own version of my spat with Madame Semprún. As each one heated up and thankfully passed, solved in some fashion, I was right back where I started.

Of all the trips I supervised, possibly the most dramatic eruption was in Houston, where I was helping manage George H. W. Bush's first G7 Economic Summit at Rice University on July 9, 1990.

Even today, I am not sure of the reasons for the conflict or why a group of Richard Nixon stalwarts was in charge of arrangements. Whatever the reason, I had to deal with them, and they guarded their territory like junkyard dogs.

For me, it was the usual assignment—to bring some semblance of order to chaos that looked good on the planners' charts but was in reality an invitation to worldwide embarrassment if anything went wrong.

Advance work is filled with battles, hurdles, and irritations. There is simply too much to be done in too little time. But at the end of a near-clockwork-perfect event, I always drew great satisfaction at meeting the challenges. I was fine with the agita by the time I had left the Reagan administration and was on the job for George H. W. Bush. I knew what to expect and dealt with it.

Most conflicts were metaphorical not physical. My battle with Madame Semprún at El Pardo Palace was one of wills, of the injection of modernity into her hallowed sanctuary to Francisco Franco. I understood her motivations and eventually learned of her Machiavellian methods to try to sabotage my first operation.

She nearly succeeded, but I had put my head down and made it through. It was a good lesson to learn as I started out.

When the Reagan administration departed, there were no fond farewell dinners or gifts of appreciation from Ron or Nancy, or anyone else for that matter. I had not expected any. I worked for them, and they left. I was an employee, not a friend. Sensitive egos don't sit well with advance work. Needy advance men don't last long.

I was prepared and glad to be back at it again with the man who in some small way had sparked my new career. I was excited to be working for President Bush, this time not as a volunteer but as a full-time staffer. I genuinely liked George H. W. Bush, a warm and compassionate man who made everyone on his staff feel welcome and valuable.

By 1990 I was as battled hardened as a combat-weary gunnery sergeant, or at least I thought I was. I had been promoted to deputy director of advance and was back to where I started out in Williamsburg—making arrangements in Bush's adopted hometown to welcome the leaders of France, West Germany, Italy, Japan, the United Kingdom, and Canada.

I would make two trips to Houston, first as head of the survey under Director of Advance John G. Keller, a man I enjoyed working with a great deal. I spent more than a week in Houston before the July G7, reviewing proposed venues and setting up as smooth a schedule as possible.

There was some pressure. Houston had become George H. W. Bush's adopted hometown, and he wanted a Texas touch to welcome the world's leaders. So attracted to Houston, at the time a growing and ostentatious oil town so different from the understated Greenwich, Connecticut, of his roots, Bush had made the Houstonian Hotel his official residence; it became his second White House. The Houstonian, settled in the woods outside the city center, had an expansive health club and a stunning golf course. He loved it there.

Houston had loved him back and enjoyed basking in the presidential glow. City leaders were enamored of Bush and the attention the summit would bring, and would spend close to $20 million on civic beautification projects before the leaders arrived.

I did not want the spotlight on mistakes, because mistakes draw the attention of the world media.

Among the events I was charged with setting up to bathe world leaders in Texan culture were a barbecue; a rodeo that would feature bull riding, barrel racing, calf scrambling, cowboys, and

Indians; oil rigs; square dancing; a sheriff with silver spurs; and a model of the space shuttle. Whether they wanted it or not, the leaders would chow down on barbecue fare that needed 1,250 gallons of sauce and jalapeños, blended with 500 pounds of onions.

The main meetings would be held at prestigious Rice University, one of the best schools in the country, though often overlooked when discussions of top schools always turned to the Ivy League.

Leaders would discuss many objectives that are still on the table as I write this in 2023, including the international economic situation; reform in Central Europe; the Soviet Union; the growing international drug problem; and the need to fight climate change, restore the ozone layer, protect biodiversity, and restore forests.

My survey report and recommendations completed and accepted, I returned to Houston eight days before the summit was to begin to dot all the *I*'s and cross all the *T*'s.

It should have been a simple task.

I had known before I began planning that the executive committee for the G7 in Houston was made up of old Nixon advance men, a group that had put a hard edge on American protocol when dealing with foreign leaders like those who would be coming to Houston. I had been surprised, since Nixon's influence had faded substantially after Watergate. I am still not sure why they were able to wield such power more than fifteen years later. Political favors run deep, I know, and whatever the reason, I was not inclined to investigate. One of the first rules I learned as I began my advance career is that the people deemed important speak only to others in their orbit. The rest are there to serve them. I was not important. I kept quiet.

Any G7 is an invasion of the host city. The teams accompanying the world leaders, the security concerns, and the media coverage can be overwhelming. I knew as I headed back to Houston for the main event, I would be part of it.

With so many people, and such tight security, it was important to assure that the Bush people had access to the various venues. To make things as simple as possible, the executive committee issued pins. Without a pin, anyone trying to gain entry to an event would be promptly given the boot. It was a simple solution to an age-old problem.

Or so I thought.

George Bush was in Europe with his team. I was in Houston with the cocky Nixon people, who treated the allocation of security pins as if they held the secret of eternal life. No pin, no access.

I broached the subject of the pins with a member of the committee, an abrasive sort of guy who made the hair on the back of my neck stand up. I did not like him or his attitude, but I approached in the most diplomatic manner I could summon.

"We need thirty-five pins," I said.

"Can't have them," he replied. "You get fifteen, the same as every other country."

"We're the host," I replied. "We need thirty-five."

"No," he said.

I detected a slight smile.

With the Bush people still in Europe, my proven strategy of kicking a conflict upstairs was impotent. We were at a standstill.

The tension, at least my tension, continued for two more days. I was seething but powerless. My Nixon counterpart stood by the rules. This was worse than the El Pardo situation.

I turned to my boss, John Keller.

"Tell the guy to give you thirty-five pins, that we insist on it and that we'll take it all the way to George Bush if we have to," he told me over the phone.

Thus armed, I walked abruptly into a meeting of the executive committee.

Without prelude or even a slight appearance of politeness, I looked at my Nixon nemesis.

"We need thirty-five pins."

"Says who?" he replied. Then he stood up quickly from his chair and leaned over the table as ten others watched.

What he said next was incredulous.

"I am an expert in kung fu. Want some?"

It was of course a ridiculous response. Jaws dropped and papers shuffled. The silence was deafening.

At the time, I held a black belt in tae kwon do, and as I stood there across the table, I was ready to use it.

I'm fairly certain that if Madame Semprún and I had gone to the mat, I would have taken her. She was in her dotage and weighed at most 110 pounds. The guy across the table from me in Houston was bigger and more adamant about protecting his turf.

I had no doubts about him either. I just didn't want to go there.

Cooler heads prevailed.

Another committee member had the presence of mind to ask on whose authority I was requesting the thirty-five pins.

My kung fu adversary continued to stare at me from across the table, then sat down.

"We'll go right to George Bush if you want, but John Keller," I said.

"Get it done."

They did.

The staid foreign leaders let their hair down and whooped it up, Texas style. Community leaders loved the attention, and George Bush relished showing the vibrant Houston culture and prestigious Rice University to the world.

The Houston G7 went off as planned.

I was certainly relieved as I packed and prepared to head home yet again.

CHAPTER 17

Yorba Linda

PACKING MY BAGS AT THE HOUSTONIAN AFTER GEORGE BUSH introduced Texas to the world, I was wiped out. My weeks-long adrenaline surge, amped up further after the bizarre kung fu experience, had evaporated. I wanted nothing more than to head home and relax for a few days with Gail before jumping back into the maelstrom.

The phone rang and, despite my inclinations, I answered.

It was John Keller.

"I need you in California tomorrow," he told me.

"I want a break, John. I need to go home."

"You don't need to do anything, Judd. You're going to Yorba Linda for the Nixon Library dedication. We need our people there."

I liked John Keller. He was a great boss and a student of the crosswinds that always inject themselves into anything political. His father had been in the US government and, like me, he was a longtime Washingtonian. He was a master of the game, and he knew the library dedication in Nixon's childhood hometown would be viewed by many of his longtime aides—all of the same ilk and rabid dedication as my kung fu master—would see the dedication as the high point of Nixon's redemption tour, which had been slowly growing for years.

They would make sure the bright lights stayed on Nixon.

"We have to protect our interests, the president's interests," he told me.

He did not have to add that if we didn't have Bush people at the dedication, which would be widely covered by the media, my dear friends in the Nixon camp would find a way to steamroll George Bush, who would attend the dedication along with former Republican presidents Gerald Ford and Ronald Reagan.

Jimmy Carter claimed he had a prior commitment. Politicians have long memories.

Keller knew, as did I, that the Nixon folks, if they had the chance, would make sure George Bush looked like a lost orphan while the spotlight shone on their man, who at the time was resuscitating his tarnished image. That's what Nixon guys did.

I called Gail, told her I wasn't coming home, and grabbed a red-eye to Los Angeles. I wasn't the only Bush advance guy to have his plans disrupted in Houston. The entire White House advance team, the communications guys, and Secret Service were all headed to Yorba Linda, where Nixon would be joined by George Bush, Ronald Reagan, Gerald Ford, and a Who's Who of Nixon administration stalwarts and an expected huge crowd of adoring Nixon supporters.

The Nixon team, bristling with testosterone, brought their A-Team, led by Ron Walker, the godfather of Nixon's no-nonsense, no-weakness approach to meetings with foreign leaders. A former Army Ranger in Vietnam, Walker kept his abrasiveness under control, but I knew it was lurking just below the surface. The library dedication would be Nixon's widest exposure since the Watergate scandal had driven him from office sixteen years before.

Walker was not about to let George Bush, Ronald Reagan, or Gerald Ford steal one reflected ray of light from his former boss.

It was only natural, then, that he viewed the Bush advance team as intruders, rude party-crashers who had to be put in their proper places before they got any ideas.

I do not believe it was a coincidence, but John Keller had assigned Ron Walker's daughter, Lisa, a stellar advance worker with an exemplary record, to the Yorba Linda team. It was a shrewd move, played by a grand master. Having her working with us, Keller felt, might temper some of Ron Walker's expected wrath.

A broiling sunshine did not deter a crowd of some fifty thousand who attended the two-and-a-half-hour dedication ceremony that included three brass bands and red-suited trumpeters to welcome the former presidents with a blaring fanfare.

In his speech, Nixon told the crowd, "Nothing we have ever seen matches this moment—to be welcomed home again."

I had much to do before the actual ceremony, but this was the crux of my visit, and I knew that before Nixon addressed it. The unstated subtext was that no one else, certainly not the upstart George Bush, would interfere with the moment. Nixon's men would make sure of that.

I caught a few hours' sleep at my hotel in Anaheim and made the twenty-minute drive to Yorba Linda early the next morning. I was dead tired.

I parked and scanned the hill and the path that led to the $21-million library, which sat near the wooden farmhouse Nixon's father had built from a kit a few years before Nixon was born in 1913. Nixon's wife, Pat, would be buried there in 1993; Nixon, a year later.

It was already hot as hell, and I hoped we would not have any sort of conflict with the Nixon people that would make it any hotter.

I had thought I'd be meeting only Ron Walker, but as I reached the top of the hill, I saw Walker along with ten other Nixon acolytes standing in line in front of the library. They looked like an ominous honor guard.

I made my way along the line, introducing myself each time. My genial handshake was met in kind by what seemed to be a concentrated effort by the ten men with Walker to crush my outreached hand.

No one said a thing, but their message was clear: This is our game. Be careful.

I was not surprised.

I worked my way to Ron Walker, who stood like the pope at the end of the line.

His first comment was clear, if puzzling: "If you think you're getting a picture taken with all five presidents together. . . . You're not."

I was not there for souvenirs.

Then Walker added something I thought redundant, given the lack of ambience if not open hostility I met as I walked up the line.

"You're going to play the game our way."

I made a mental note to tell my staff to be very careful, but to make sure George Bush was not flattened. I wanted everyone on the Bush advance team to take great pains to be polite but to remain assertive. I did not want a scene.

After the meeting on the hill, one of Walker's minions gave me a tour of the impressive facility, a tribute to Nixon's long and storied career as a California congressman, senator, and two-term vice president under Dwight Eisenhower.

He had done much good, I thought as I toured the library, but he simply could not control his inner demons.

My job in Yorba Linda was not to remind anyone of Nixon's darker side. No one among the throngs of admirers needed a reminder. The next few days were meant as a celebration of his accomplishments. My job was to prevent George Bush from appearing to be an uninvited guest.

We did that.

It was not easy, though.

Back at the Hilton in Anaheim after a full day of site planning, I got a call from Ron Walker. Despite his outward aggression, I liked him. I knew he was a good man who was trying to protect Nixon on his long-awaited return. He had worked for Nixon for years, I knew, and I understood.

Walker wasted no time on pleasantries.

"What do you and your smart-ass boss, John G. Keller, think you're doing assigning my daughter to this event?"

"Ron," I said, "Lisa is one of our top aides. She is here because she is a damn good advance," I told him. "She's here because we need her."

Silence. Then he hung up.

I can only assume he felt he had to make his point, that he was watching and was not oblivious to Keller's machinations.

The fact is, though, Walker's men went out of their way to accommodate Lisa and do whatever she requested. I'm sure the Nixon team members felt extra pressure, knowing that upsetting one of Ron Walker's family members would not be a good idea. I never asked her, but I assume she did not get any bone-crushing handshakes.

She did a great job, and, frankly, John Keller had played the cards dealt to him with flair and prescience. It could have easily gone south, given the near-open hostility from the Nixon team.

The dedication was flawless.

I had only one moment of startling anxiety during George Bush's address to a gathering that included Nixon's man for all seasons, Henry Kissinger, and former secretaries of state William Rogers, George P. Shultz, and Alexander Haig.

During his speech, which was full of praise and admiration for Nixon's accomplishments, Bush mentioned Watergate.

I nearly had a major coronary.

Bush had his reasons.

As head of the Republican National Committee in 1974, Bush, as Nixon's fate was becoming more apparent, distanced himself from Nixon's defenders and called for Nixon's resignation, noting that, "I would now ill-serve a president, whose massive accomplishments I will always respect, and whose family I love, if I did not give you my judgment. Resignation is best for this country, best for this president."

In his address, Bush made great effort to praise Nixon's accomplishments, but he added one remark that none of the other luminaries dared mention.

People who visited the library, he told the crowd of admirers, "will hear of Horatio Alger and Alger Hiss. Of his book *Six Crises* and the seventh crisis, Watergate."

I nearly choked, but the remark went unnoticed by most of the crowd.

Frankly, I thought it was appropriate.

That was as close as we would come to what could have been an eighth crisis if the Nixon folk had taken umbrage.

They did not.

Another assignment was finished, and I was exhausted. I had not been home for eighteen days.

CHAPTER 18

George H. W. Bush in Egypt

THE MIDDLE EAST WAS ON THE VERGE OF EXPLODING IN NOVEM-
ber 1990 and a determined George H. W. Bush intended to keep
the sparks under control. One misunderstanding, one misinter-
pretation of American intentions, real or imagined, would have
catastrophic consequences.

For George Bush, it was another day at the office. For me, it
meant I was in Cairo for several days to prepare for his meeting
with Egyptian President Hosni Mubarak.

The tensions were palpable, and abrupt alterations of the president's hectic schedule were expected. On this trip, last-minute
detours were certain. It was all part of my day.

I had the good fortune of knowing the American ambassador
to Egypt, Frank Wisner Jr. A good friend, Wisner was a longtime
Washington insider who would go on to serve as under secretary
of state for international security affairs. He was the son of a leg-
endary clandestine services operative at the CIA.

One can never underestimate the value of contacts in the
advance business.

Shortly after I arrived, Wisner pulled me aside during a meeting at the Cairo Marriott and told me that a top-secret meeting
between George Bush and Syrian strongman Hafez al-Assad, a

longtime antagonist of the United States, had just been arranged. The meeting was vastly important to Bush's coalition-building mission to the Middle East that month. Bush had recently named Syria a major supporter of international terrorism, and bringing Assad into the fold would be a major accomplishment.

A meeting between the two was big news. If George Bush could add Syria to the list of coalition allies he was assembling after Iraq had invaded and taken control of neighboring Kuwait, an announcement would be a diplomatic coup.

"They'll meet in either Geneva or Cyprus," Wisner told me.

"Nobody knows about this. You need to call Keller."

Calling John Keller, who was with Bush in Saudi Arabia and about to head to Cairo, meant that there was little or no time for any advance work, a secure room, Secret Service coverage, or communications setups.

Preparations for the meeting between Bush and Assad had to be ad-libbed. We jury-rigged a SCIF in the hotel bathroom with mattresses, and I called Keller and woke him up.

Keller was not a man given to niceties when he was rousted.

"What do you want? This better be good."

I told him, beginning another circus of last-minute scrambling to accommodate the backchannel historic meeting between Bush and Assad, which took place two days later in Geneva, with Syria joining Bush's coalition.

I still had to tend to Bush's meeting with Mubarak in Egypt, where seams and layers of intrigue were abundant. I recalled once hearing the world of espionage and international relations described as a wilderness of mirrors, where nothing seemed as it appeared, and intentions were never what they were professed to be.

Distrust was everywhere, and I was in the middle of it.

There was much madness on that short trip.

In August 1990, three months before I arrived in Cairo with my team, elite Iraqi troops under Saddam Hussein had invaded its oil-rich neighbor, Kuwait, and in two days were in full control. It was the beginning of seven months of chaos, with the rest of the world carefully watching and planning.

The world's oil reserves were at stake. Ensconced in Kuwait, the Iraqi army could easily launch an equally brazen attack on Saudi Arabian oil fields just across the border. With Saddam Hussein, anything was possible. Kuwait and the Saudi oil fields in hand, Saddam would control most of the world's reserves.

It was an unsettling prospect.

The United States would lead a coalition of United Nations forces in a two-phase effort that began immediately after Saddam's invasion of Kuwait, with US forces engaged in what became known as Operation Desert Shield, a buildup of troops intended to protect Saudi Arabia and ultimately dislodge Iraqi troops from Kuwait.

In November, George Bush set out on a trip to assure Middle Eastern players that America's intentions were honorable, its ability to bring the crisis to end efficient, and the results for all involved positive.

It was, as we used to say in the hotel business, a hard sell.

George Bush proved correct in his assumptions about the end. Coalition forces led by the United States would make short work of its own invasion of Iraq beginning in August, Operation Desert Storm. Five weeks later, at the end of February, the conflict ended victoriously for the coalition, and a cease-fire agreement was signed.

In Iraq, with its cauldron of competing interests, a revolution would break out. Saddam Hussein would prevail and would again insert himself as leader. He was not finished, of course. Thirteen years later he would test the will of another president—and another Bush. George H. W. Bush's son, George W. Bush, for whom I would also work.

I'm not certain if my time in Egypt in 1990 prepared me for the second Iraq War, but it did give me a taste of the volatile politics of the Middle East.

George H. W. Bush would arrive in Cairo from Saudi Arabia on November 22 to meet with Mubarak. The problems began before he disembarked Air Force One.

I arrived the day before for a walk-though of every building, office, and corridor the president would visit. Tensions were high. The Egyptians were, at least on the surface, pro-American and supported Desert Shield. But it is a mistake to view any country and any people as a homogeneous society, to paint them with the same brush. Generalities in foreign relations are a dangerous assumption that has led to more than one war.

Mubarak was pro-American at the time, a member of the allied coalition; though within Egypt, there were others who disagreed. We had to be careful while George Bush was in Cairo. The Secret Service was on high alert, and for me that added more tension.

The Egyptian leadership was a high-wire act for the principals. Being Egyptian president was not a job for the faint of heart. Mubarak had served as Anwar Sadat's vice president from 1975 until 1981. When Sadat was assassinated in 1981, Mubarak became president and would serve in that position for close to thirty years.

I was nervous.

On the surface, my Egyptian counterparts were cooperative and helpful, but I had learned early in my career that meant nothing. On one hand, I was given access to survey Mubarak's office for as long as I wanted, and I did, checking that everything would meet the rigorous security standards for his one-one-one meeting with George Bush.

One the other hand, I knew that while I was in Mubarak's office, my hotel room was being searched and my hotel phone was tapped, not that I planned on using it.

My antenna was up.

After leaving Mubarak's office, I had my driver take me to the American embassy, where I expressed my concerns to the regional security officer there. He knew. Mine was a redundant effort, but I preferred redundancy to expediency. The regional security officer assured me that all contingencies had been covered. He had spoken to the Secret Service, who were equally on edge.

My next stop was the Cairo Marriott, where the president would overnight. We had reserved an entire floor, the better to control. We stationed a US Marine guard at every place of entry, including the elevators and stairwells. No one would be admitted without proper documentation, which included top-secret clearances. We set up a SCIF in one of the rooms—which I had used to inform John Keller about the Assad meeting—and stationed a Marine guard at the door.

We were taking no chances. It was the most intensive security arrangement I had supervised on any presidential trip. Still, I knew enough to not breathe a sigh of relief just yet.

The president had not yet arrived.

When he did, all hell would break loose.

I arrived at Cairo International Airport five hours before George Bush and Air Force One would arrive from Saudi Arabia at ten o'clock that evening. I had a long meeting with my staff before I headed out, drilling into them once again the strict rules for a presidential arrival. Protocol drove everything, and certain steps must be followed meticulously.

Air Force One carried not only the president but also military and staff aides, State Department advisors, Secret Service agents, a large press following, and the crew. The large aircraft can carry as many as seventy passengers.

Everyone aboard had been briefed on the protocol of disembarking, with the president always the first to leave Air Force One. Without rules in place, exiting the plane would be no different from the usual scramble, elbowing, and aisle-blocking dance following any normal commercial flight.

Protocol for an Air Force One landing demanded patience and, for some aboard, a rare exercise of courtesy.

Normally, once off the plane, passengers would head for the motorcade and their assigned cars, which I had arranged, with twenty-five waiting cars parked precisely, doors open and waiting. If it's pulled off properly, passengers are off the plane and on their way with the flair of a well-executed touchdown pass.

Waiting for Air Force One to arrive, I checked that everything was in place, cars waiting.

It was getting dark.

A half hour before the anticipated landing, I noticed an Egyptian military figure ordering that the cars be moved. I approached and noticed he was a general. He had given the drivers no specific destinations, only that they move. No car was where it was supposed to be, and no one leaving the plane would have any idea where they were supposed to go.

I quickly envisioned a chaotic "welcome to Cairo" scene, not the best first step for the president or anyone else.

I approached the general.

"You can't do this."

"This is my country, my airport, my tarmac," he said.

I knew I'd get nowhere.

I immediately called John Keller, who was aboard Air Force One as it approached.

"I'm afraid I've lost control of the airport," I said.

Keller was not a man to waste words or offer sympathy.

"What the hell is going on?"

I explained the situation, feeling my earpiece melting in my ear as Keller continued to berate me. The calmest response I got from him was that he would inform the president, then the passengers.

I'm not sure how they worked it out in the short time they had before landing, but they did.

Bush left the plane and was whisked away safely. The remaining passengers, alerted to the problem, did not meander looking for their cars but instead waited while the rest of the motorcade assembled and left for the town, none the worse for the interruption.

I'd later catch a lot of grief for that, but Keller, despite his inherent edginess, understood that the situation was not my fault.

I never learned why the mysterious general had intervened. Sometimes it's best not to pry.

I would connect again with Frank Wisner shortly before I left. He was a good friend of my uncle Smith Hempstone, then serving as US ambassador to Kenya. Wisner and my uncle made strange bedfellows, the career diplomat and the outspoken journalist. Wisner and I used the secure phone in the embassy to talk to my uncle, share a few laughs, and drink in the strange set of coincidences that had drawn us together so far from our Washington roots.

In what was perhaps one of my oddest detours, I attended a service at the American Episcopal Church with Frank Wisner shortly before I left Cairo. I had not been to church for some time. It provided a short meditative moment I needed and relished. That I was in a large Christian church in one of the most populous Muslim cities in the world fit in with the theme.

I found that the experience offered much comfort in a world on the brink.

CHAPTER 19

Staying in the Game

SAME GAME, DIFFERENT TITLE.

I developed other plans and moved on after George H. W. Bush left the White House. The shelf life of any career tied to politics is short, and anyone who's been there either knows that or will learn quickly.

If the chads hadn't hung, if they had fallen in Al Gore's favor, I still would have been fine.

Eight years after George H. W. Bush boarded Marine One and flew to Andrews Air Force Base for his flight home to Houston, two hellish, contentious, and agonizing weeks in Florida put his son in office, and I would go along with him. My new job for the George W. Bush administration arrived after a circuitous tour.

I'd still be planning important meetings in the Bush administration, still be attending to the countless details and dealing with over-the-top egos, but I'd be doing it as a deputy assistant secretary for international affairs for fossil fuels at the US Department of Energy. I did not say goodbye to presidential advance, though. Because I held top-secret/sensitive compartmented clearances, I was still called on by the White House to run especially delicate trips made by George W. Bush.

Still ahead were the showdown at Putin's dacha, an emotionally wrenching trip to Auschwitz, riots in Genoa, a meeting in Shanghai with Putin at a hotel so full of wiretaps it's a wonder we didn't trip over them, and a close encounter with the Shining Path guerrillas in Peru.

My return after Bill Clinton left office, I suppose, also involved a little bit of luck and the good graces of some Al Gore supporters.

The contentious 2000 election between George W. Bush and Al Gore came down to Florida, where, as election results trickled in, Gore was at first declared the national winner by some media. Shortly before the polls closed in Florida, votes from its heavily Republican Panhandle would change that. Networks amended their assessment, next saying it was "too close to call," later followed by the announcement that Bush had won. It was not a golden moment for television pundits.

The confusion would continue when Gore conceded but then changed his mind and demanded a Florida recount.

Nothing like that had ever happened in a presidential election.

I was in Florida during the laborious and exhausting recount process, working for the Bush campaign. There was nothing polite about the recount, as teams of Bush and Gore folks elbowed each other, literally and figuratively, to make sure each vote was properly tallied.

Votes would be recounted by hand, which set the stage for a tense few weeks that looked more like the Shootout at the OK Corral than a dignified and controlled effort to determine the next president.

At the core of the recount tensions were ballots that had been deemed incomplete and thus uncounted because the voting machine had not completely punched through a chosen candidate's name on the paper ballot, a failure that brought "hanging chad" into the American lexicon.

In the end, my future career in politics depended on the graciousness of some Gore operatives who opted to look the other way when, in an imprudent moment I still don't regret, I decked one of their obnoxious colleagues—an atavistic reaction from my long-ago days as a military policeman. He was too close to me and too antagonistic, and I flat out popped him with a right hook. It was an indelicate but well-deserved reaction that lacked the tact and diplomacy I had practiced for years in advance work.

In Florida, I was no longer in the business of tact and diplomacy. I was in a war zone. The guy deserved it.

I suspect the Gore people had wanted to do the same to their obnoxious colleague. My pugilism was never mentioned again, and I moved on.

George W. Bush prevailed in the recount that made my intemperate outburst moot.

That's how things work in Washington.

Washington politics is an odd game of reinvention, the comforting embrace of long memories, and the fragile hope that your record of achievement had been noted by those in power. There is no place in the entire world where "What have you done for me lately?" is used with greater frequency.

Apparently, what I had done in my years as an advance man was good.

After George H. W. Bush left office, I carved a new career, satisfied I had done the best I could.

In my new post-advance work, I would end up at the nexus of some very tense but often celebratory gatherings doing what I had always done, making sessions run as smoothly as possible, this time as a private citizen.

It was an odd path but, in Washington, perfectly normal.

Saying goodbye to my old advance job was bittersweet. In politics, such goodbyes are not unexpected, and I was prepared when George H. W. Bush lost to Bill Clinton in 1992.

After the election, there were only a few of us left in Washington to tend to the details of helping the Clintons move into the White House from Blair House, across Pennsylvania Avenue, where they were staying temporarily.

George H. W. Bush, gracious in defeat, had gathered me, presidential assistant Peggy Hazelrigg, Director of Press Advance John Herrick, and Press Secretary Marlin Fitzwater to attend to details.

"Make sure you treat the Clintons and their staff with the utmost respect—and make sure they get everything they want."

I had no problem with that. George H. W. Bush treated everyone that way.

Then he turned to me.

"You'll be the last man standing."

I had no problem with that either.

I was not surprised to see that Bush and Clinton became good friends in later years.

I worked with Hillary Clinton's top aide Kelly Craighead during the transition, and together we attended to the myriad details of the move without too many hitches.

As always, there were a few. I did have one reminder that my old job had not always been a bed of roses. Standing on the White House steps as the inaugural motorcade assembled, a man I recognized as a new Clinton cabinet member approached.

He obviously mistook me for a Clinton guy.

"Where's my car?"

"I don't know," I replied, perhaps too nonchalantly. Truth is, I could have added, "and I don't care."

"Bullshit," he shouted. "Find my car."

I noticed a Washington police department cruiser idling nearby, led the man to it, and guided him to the back seat. Then I told the officer inside to take the man to the Capitol Building. The angry soon-to-be cabinet member scowled at me, looking like a perp on the way to lockup. I'm sure that was not how he had imagined his entry into the inner circle would begin.

I would not miss that attitude. I had seen it all too often—the arrogance that comes with power, real or imagined.

When George H. W. Bush boarded Marine One, I went home and cried in my beer.

Then I moved on.

I felt that my years as a White House advance man who knew how to stage events, with a background in hotels, and a good understanding of how to manage media, would turn heads. And it did.

I founded J. R. Swift and Associates, and with the contacts I had developed over the years, I curated a strong list of clients hoping for an inside edge in Washington, among them Lawrence Livermore Laboratories; the prestigious law firm and lobbying group, Baker, Donelson, Bearman, Caldwell & Berkowitz; and Phillip Morris, then moving from its controversial tobacco focus into other investments in Kraft Foods and Miller Beer.

I knew from my years as a Washington insider that if I wanted to get the things done required by my clients, I had to reach out to the career people, the men and women in various agencies who had made policy their life work. They were invested in making things happen and knew how to accomplish it. Career people believe in government and its utility.

I avoided the political people, the appointees whose main motivation was self-interest. They are disinclined to focus on a policy that might take years to develop and be approved. Their concerns rested only on the moment and how they looked. To them, policy was ephemeral, annoying, and time consuming.

The career people are the backbone of democracy; I knew many of them and respected them and what they did, regardless of the political flavor of the administration in power.

Baker Donelson was led by former Tennessee Senator Howard Baker, who rose to fame during the Watergate hearings. An influential partner was Lawrence Eagleburger, who served briefly as secretary of state under George H. W. Bush, and had worked for Richard Nixon, Jimmy Carter, and Ronald Reagan.

I had met Eagleburger years before through my uncle Smith Hempstone, further proof of the value of contacts in the closed world of Washington.

I loved Lawrence Eagleburger.

A tribute to his effectiveness and his ability to avoid the maelstrom of partisan politics was that when Eagleburger died in 2011, Barack Obama described him as a "distinguished diplomat and public servant who devoted his life to the security of our nation and to strengthening our ties with allies and partners."

With J. R. Swift and Associates, I would travel the world once again in my new incarnation, enjoying the challenges. But I kept an eye on Washington and kept in touch with former colleagues.

When George W. Bush began attracting attention as a possible presidential candidate, I wrote to his father that I'd be delighted to help his son in any way I could.

Successful politics, deadly at times and vicious, can be distilled in its most basic form to trust. The same trusted players emerge in different positions because candidates know their loyalty is unquestioned. It leaves more time to attend to getting elected and less time worrying about backdoor perfidies.

I was a beneficiary of that philosophy, certainly. George H. W. Bush trusted me and said as much to his son. He wrote a very nice note to George W. Bush recommending me.

I received a nice reply from George W. Bush inviting me to come down to Austin, Texas, where the George W. Bush campaign was amping up his presidential bid. There, I would assist his campaign advance man, Brian Montgomery, who I would work closely with.

My reentry into presidential work was percolating. I was being pulled back in and found it a pleasant experience. I had missed being in the game.

Montgomery was an example of political trust. He had worked for George W. Bush for years in Texas when Bush was a rising political star. The two were close. Montgomery would be beside Bush on September 11, 2001, when the president, as he read to elementary schoolchildren, would be told that the World Trade Center and Pentagon had been attacked.

When George W. Bush won the Republican primary for president over a packed field that included Arizona Senator John McCain, financier Steve Forbes, Utah Senator Orrin Hatch, and former NBA star and New Jersey Senator Bill Bradley, he named Dick Cheney as his vice presidential running mate.

Brian Montgomery assigned me to serve as Dick Cheney's director of operations.

Montgomery asked me to assist with the Cheney campaign, running one of five teams coordinating Cheney's schedule at campaign stops around the country. Dick Cheney was and remains a controversial figure, a man known for his Machiavellian intrigues. I felt at the time, and still do, that despite his darker side, he was what George W. Bush—and the country—needed during those fragile months. The country was reeling after September 11, under siege. Diplomacy had proved impotent against terrorism, and extreme measures were called for. Cheney knew that, and he had George W. Bush's ear.

Dick Cheney was always prepared for anything, and I rarely saw him without a briefing book in his face, studying. He was always up to date. He did what he thought was needed.

My work with Dick Cheney had once again brought me back into the stream, pulled along by the excitement. George W. Bush by then had established his own advance team, but I was invited to join the Department of Energy, once again traveling the world, supervising sensitive meetings, dealing with the press, and managing the message of the Bush administration's international push to move new energy technologies into the developing world.

The job was fraught with intrigue because, in many instances, energy meant nuclear, and nuclear at times meant weapons. Weapons in the wrong hands meant trouble.

It was an interesting job, to say the least. I loved it.

Once again, I'd find myself sitting in the back of an airplane, headed off to somewhere important people would negotiate important matters.

But I had not seen the end of my presidential advance work. Vladimir Putin, the pope, and the Shining Path were waiting.

CHAPTER 20

9/11 Pentagon Commemoration

THE CALL PRESENTED A WRENCHING IRONY.

On one hand, the president wanted me back to tend to a multitude of advance details after I'd been away for eight years. On the other, I would have done anything to erase the reason for George W. Bush's request. I would have gladly foresworn presidential politics, advance work, the allure of power plays, and the reflected spotlight in Washington I enjoyed so much.

I did not want to oversee and coordinate the White House's plans for the one-year commemoration of the most cataclysmic and wrenching event in the history of the United States.

George W. Bush would address relatives of those killed, high-ranking military, and service members from a stage erected just below the wall of the Pentagon that had been obliterated the year before by hijacked American Airlines Flight 77.

Bush's address would be a sorrowful reminder of the tragedy and a call to action to prevent the horrors of September 11, 2001, from ever happening again. I wished there were no need for such a somber, heartbreaking commemoration.

After I accepted the invitation to handle the details, I knew the entire country would be watching. There was no room for error or carelessness.

I had stepped away from advance work and the White House after Bill Clinton was elected in 1992. But once baptized into the world of Washington politics, one never strays too far from the cathedral.

With the election of George W. Bush in 2000, I was back in orbit. Still drawn to the game and still connected, I had been asked to work for the Department of Energy, and at that point further White House advance work was not in the cards.

In early September 2002, Brian Montgomery, a George W. Bush favorite I had come to know over the years, called and asked me to step away from my Department of Energy duties and coordinate the solemn memorial ceremony at the Pentagon. Montgomery had been beside Bush on September 11, 2001, when Bush was informed that the World Trade Center in New York had been attacked. We would soon learn those attacks were part of a coordinated suicide effort carried out by the extremist militant network al-Qaeda against the United States.

Close to three thousand Americans who had begun their workweeks that brilliant sunny day with optimism and hope were killed.

George W. Bush's speech on September 11, 2002, would honor the 64 people aboard American Airlines Flight 77 and the 125 at work in the Pentagon who died.

The eyes of the entire country would be on the gathering outside the Pentagon. Americans were looking to George W. Bush for consolation and leadership, for any sign that we would be fine, that the cretins who had done this would pay for it.

The ceremony and the coverage of it had to be perfect.

I had one week.

I was honored. I knew immediately that everything about the ceremony and George W. Bush's role in it had to be flawlessly executed. I was confident I would pull it off but, at the same time, was aware that I had never been under more pressure.

In September 2002 I was still seething, angry beyond human understanding, over the terrorist attacks on the World Trade Center and the Pentagon, and of United Airlines Flight 93, whose intended target was the US Capitol Building but ultimately crashed near Shanksville, Pennsylvania, killing forty-four heroic passengers.

I love my country. I had served it proudly as a military policeman in the US Army and had dedicated eight years to helping George H. W. Bush and Ronald Reagan.

I was both outraged and saddened by those attacks.

The precise moment I learned of the attacks in New York, followed shortly by the one at the Pentagon, not even three miles from my office, is acid-etched into my psyche—much the same way the assassination of John F. Kennedy and the news of the bombing of Pearl Harbor are for millions of Americans. Even today, more than twenty years later, a certain smell, a song I heard on the radio driving in that morning, a peculiar glint of light off an office window, can send me back to the instant I heard.

I cannot unsee those towers crumbling.

September 11, 2001, I had been sitting in my office at the Department of Energy, beside Washington Mall on Independence Avenue, not three miles from the Pentagon across the Potomac in Arlington, Virginia. I had arrived at work but never began, horrified and distracted by the news of what could possibly have been a terrorist attack at the World Trade Center in New York City. Shortly after 9:30, I noticed black smoke rising from across the Potomac River.

I knew instantaneously that the attacks in New York and Washington were related.

I left for home immediately, as did everyone in the building. Secretary of Energy Spencer Abraham and senior staff were flown to a secret location.

"We are at war," I told my staff as I left for home and Gail.

We lived in Arlington at the time, and I drove past the Pentagon on my way home. Fire trucks, emergency personnel, and special military units were swarming the area. A perimeter of armed guards had been set up. Security was airtight, and for good reason. No one knew what was happening.

Gail met me at our front door, horrified. We hugged but said nothing.

For a year, I would drive by the Pentagon on my way to the Department of Energy.

A year later, Brian Montgomery called.

"We need you for the Pentagon memorial service, Judd," he said. I knew I would do it, and I knew I did not have to clear a week's absence with my bosses at the Department of Energy. When a president says he needs you, you jump.

Because of the potential for another terrorist attack at the open-air speech, security was at its absolute highest. The ceremony would be attended not only by George W. Bush but also such high national figures as Secretary of Defense Donald Rumsfeld. Less than a month after the attacks in 2001, George W. Bush had announced that the United States had begun military action in Afghanistan against al-Qaeda training camps and Taliban installations.

That's where I came in. Because of my previous work, and my continuing work with the Department of Energy, I had the highest security clearance possible. That would allow me to walk the tightly monitored halls of the Pentagon freely. I needed to speak to generals in a half dozen offices to assure that the memorial program went ahead without a hitch.

My first stop was the White House, where I attended a briefing led by Brian Montgomery outlining plans for the day. I left with a good sense of what was needed—and also the knowledge that Montgomery would be watching me like a hawk.

The next morning I drove to the Pentagon for a short meeting with Donald Rumsfeld, who was accommodating and helpful in getting me the proper identification to find my way through the labyrinth of Pentagon corridors.

George W. Bush would be speaking in front of a tightly controlled audience composed of families of those killed in the attack and relatives and coworkers of those on the Pentagon staff.

My job was to make sure everyone got in and out of the assembled bleachers we would set up—safely and on time.

That meant speaking to generals to clear such things as seating arrangements, transportation to and from the site for attendees, parking clearances, schedules for the arrival of VIPs, arranging optimum vantage points for media coverage and photographers, getting proper identification tags for all participants—seemingly trifling details, but all important.

Everyone listened and provided the assistance I needed with no complaint. Despite the seriousness of the occasion, I chuckled at the multi-starred generals who jumped to provide anything I asked for. As a former NCO (noncommissioned officer), I found it somewhat amusing.

One of the White House's major concerns outside the smooth arrival of the president was the construction and wiring of the stage from which dignitaries would speak. I needed to assure media access, including sound and lighting for the best possible coverage of the president's address. This meant a torrent of workers literally running around the site. Every single one had to be cleared and wearing the proper identification.

George W. Bush would deliver his address standing below a huge four-story American flag, a replica of the one unfurled by fire and rescue workers following the attack.

It was starkly beautiful and profoundly emotional to see that flag. I knew it was the perfect backdrop for the president's speech. Everything I did in the five days I ran around the Pentagon securing permissions, issuing orders, and implementing the White House plans was centered on making sure George W. Bush spoke from a podium on the dais.

He did, and it was stunning. George W. Bush's address was moving, and, as I stood below the dais, I was struck by his opening words:

> Many civilian and military personnel have now returned to offices they occupied before the attack. The Pentagon is a working building, not a memorial. Yet, the memories of a great tragedy linger here. And for all who knew loss here, life is not the same.
>
> The 184 whose lives were taken in this place—veterans and recruits, soldiers and civilians, husbands and wives, parents and children—left behind family and friends whose loss cannot be weighed. The murder of innocents cannot be explained, only endured. And though they died in tragedy, they did not die in vain. Their loss has moved a nation to action, in a cause to defend other innocent lives across the world.

I looked over the audience. Many were crying.

A week later, I received a handwritten note from Chief of Staff Andrew Card.

September 16, 2002

Dear Judd,

You did a great job making sure the 9/11 remembrance at The Pentagon went well. Thank you!

The president is fortunate to have you on his team.

Sincerely,
Andy Card

I felt fortunate to have been able to help.

I never wanted to do an event like that again.

CHAPTER 21

Genoa

NEARLY TWO HUNDRED THOUSAND DEMONSTRATORS, MORE THAN one-third of the city's population, were assembling in Genoa to greet George W. Bush and other world leaders. I knew their greeting would not be accompanied by flowers and cheers for a job well done.

The protestors' welcome was brimming with ill intent, and their aim was to send the twenty-seventh G8 Summit meeting in July 2001 off the rails.

By then, the protestors were practiced in the ways of disruption.

They had done a very good job of it in years past, upsetting meetings in London; Eugene, Oregon; and Seattle, Washington, as what become known as the "anti-globalization" movement took shape and honed its tactics.

Seattle in 1999 was particularly raucous, with protestors blocking World Trade Organization delegates from entering the city convention center, clashing with police, smashing windows, and throwing rocks. Some six hundred protestors were arrested, and thousands of others were injured.

As I and the rest of the advance survey team studied Genoa in the weeks ahead of the summit and laid out plans, we knew the protestors had improved their capability for mayhem. I knew there was nothing we could do to stop the protests, but I was determined to keep George W. Bush out of the fray.

Birthplace of Christopher Columbus, the centuries-old city in northwestern Italy along the Italian Riviera was a major maritime and shipbuilding center. With its narrow streets, Genoa was a perfect venue for chaos.

The host Italians, new to planning a major event featuring world leaders, and no doubt with a cautious eye on isolating the leaders and their parties from the protestors, had come up with a plan to have them stay on cruise ships moored in the harbor.

To the survey team, which I led along with Jeannie Bull from the State Department, who I had worked with many times, the idea was a nonstarter. We unanimously agreed that there was too much potential for serious harm. The cruise ships were sitting ducks.

We chose instead to house George Bush and the American delegation at the Jolly Hotel, which presented its own set of problems. The Jolly was a carefully restored and stunning nineteenth-century building on an old wharf in the city center, sitting on pilings near the harbor's edge. Putting the Americans at the Jolly would allow us and the Secret Service more control over security. But the Jolly, whose undersides were exposed at low tide, prompted us to bring a new set of players into our usual protection plans: a squad of US Navy SEALs.

The addition would present a front-row seat for me to observe the results of mixing the clashing machismos of the Secret Service and the SEALs, who would, by the summit's end, have the last laugh in what I would later think of as the little-known Italian Battle of Testosterone, 2001.

The twenty-seventh G8 Summit would bring together such luminaries as George Bush, Jean Chrétien of Canada, Jacques Chirac of France, Gerhard Schröder of Germany, Tony Blair of

Great Britain, Vladimir Putin of Russia, and Silvio Berlusconi of Italy. The summit's theme was reducing world poverty, a topic that was no doubt laughable to the anti-globalization protestors, who believed that growing worldwide poverty, especially in Third World nations, was due to the rise in influence of the multinational corporations at whose bidding the very leaders in Genoa served.

They saw the summit as a unique opportunity to make their point and were massing on the streets of Genoa in the days before the start of the meetings.

The Genoa summit was a perfect storm and an invitation for the chaos that ensued. From the perspective of the anti-globalists, it was not unlike hosting a three-day banquet to discuss famine initiatives.

Knowing that the summit was fraught with potential for violent disruptions, we had done a thorough and exacting survey in the weeks before. We were aware that the extremely nervous Italians had sparked controversy and media ridicule by erecting fences in the streets, even running them through city houses, which must have appalled the homeowners.

Event planners also banned hanging laundry out to dry.

To further insult residents, the organizers created a "Red Zone" surrounded by a barricade in the city center and declared it off-limits to nonresidents. To add icing to the cake, they set up jarringly out-of-place missile batteries throughout the city and established a no-fly zone over the city to prevent a possible terrorist attack.

We had been through the drill far more than the Italians and did our best to help.

The enormity of the restrictions became apparent when I arrived a few days before the summit. We could not leave the Jolly to have dinner; city residents were on edge. The police, the carabinieri, had gone off the edge days before.

They were ready to fight, an unfortunate attitude that, in retrospect, only created more tension at a time when cooler heads could have prevented much of the violence that occurred.

It was not pretty.

With our survey and completed plans in place, I returned to Genoa seven days before the summit to supervise operations at the Jolly, packed tightly into other buildings on a city-center wharf, a half mile from the cruise ships where other world leaders and their delegations were staying.

We set up the necessary communications systems and enlarged a suite to accommodate the usual large numbers of aides, policy advisors, assistants, and hangers-on.

The Italians were gracious and patient.

I walked miles on beautiful marble floors and steep stairways and found that my calves were neither gracious nor accommodating. By the eve of the summit, though, I felt we were ready for anything.

Security was paramount. Because the Jolly sat above the water at the harbor's edge, during the survey we had decided to call on the Navy SEALs to supplement the usual and always ironclad efforts provided by the Secret Service. They would work to prevent any possible underwater security breaches.

The Secret Service guys took the move as an affront. I watched carefully as the ballet between the two groups unfolded menacingly. Each no doubt had only the president's safety in mind, first and foremost. But neither thought much of the other's ability to prevent an international embarrassment.

It was an inevitable standoff.

The SEALs, as they are wont to do, arrived at the Jolly at night, four days prior to the summit's first day of sessions, surreptitiously on a dropping tide in two inflatable boats powered by rumbling six-cylinder diesel engines, and docked at the Jolly. Each boat was large enough to accommodate eight men. At low tide they would float under the Jolly and check for wires or, possibly, explosives.

They would remain in charge of checking under the hotel and keeping it secure for the duration of the summit.

I pulled the SEAL leader aside and told him that while I held the highest security clearances, I'd refrain from giving him specific instructions or, for that matter, asking what they planned to do. I knew they were good.

"Do what you have to," I said.

He seemed to respect that. I never heard from him again, and we had no problems.

The Secret Service and the SEALs met at the dock, posturing, looking like rutting elks during mating season. From my perspective on the dockside in front of the Jolly, it was humorous. The machismo was dripping.

When their survey was completed, the SEALs returned to the dock outside the ornate front doors of the hotel.

I heard the SEAL leader ask a hovering Secret Service agent if anyone wanted to tour the harbor. It was a coup of gamesmanship. Three agents jumped into the inflatable.

Those diesel-powered inflatables were capable of hitting forty knots in quick order, and, as I watched, it didn't take long to hit top speed as the inflatable burst from the dock, doing a one-eighty as soon as it cleared two nearby boats moored forty yards off the wharf. In the open water of the outer harbor it did another, then another, becoming airborne as it crossed its own wake.

I continued watching as the inflatable slowed, dropped back into the water, and returned to the dock.

Two of the Secret Service agents pulled themselves from the inflatable at the dock, stepped on solid ground, and vomited profusely.

Game. Set. Match.

Security matters were not the advance team's only concerns. As overzealous as the Italians were about preventing the rioters from emerging victorious, they were vastly unprepared in matters of protocol, the essence of any international meeting. They were new to the enormity of details involved in seating and announcing delegates, how to have them enter the negotiating rooms, how to set up multiple meetings simultaneously, and the minutia of international diplomacy. Embarrassments could easily become international incidents, and the Italians prevailed on us to help keep things running smoothly.

On the advance team in Genoa, we had Kim Barnes Kimball, a team member I valued greatly and considered the Emily Post of matters concerning protocol. Patient and knowledgeable, she went right to work with the Italian team, answering questions and directing the delicate script so necessary to managing meetings.

The Italians were ecstatic. At least one element was running properly.

Outside in the streets, however, things were turning ominous.

I felt the fences set up by the carabinieri were draconian and only served to antagonize the demonstrators. The demonstrators, though I am not entirely confident of their sincerity, had stated they only wanted to speak to the leaders about their concerns, to create some sort of meaningful dialogue. With the tight security, that was impossible and certainly increased frustration.

I had no doubt that the protestors wanted to disrupt the summit, and no doubt that the crowds would resort to violence. But crowd-control tactics in Genoa were equally as violent as that of the protestors, and the carabinieri showed little tact.

One demonstrator was killed, 329 were arrested, and dozens were hospitalized. It was an unnecessary ending to what was described by protest leaders as a "nonviolent" attempt to be heard.

That few such demonstrations occur these days is testimony to what lessons law-enforcement officials have learned.

As far as I know, the only American injury was that to the pride of two Secret Service agents.

CHAPTER 22

Shanghai

ON PAPER, IT SEEMED LIKE A BRILLIANT IDEA AT FIRST, FULL OF symbolism and hopefulness—of calm in troubled times. George W. Bush and Vladimir Putin would meet for talks at the Peace Hotel in Shanghai.

The enormous swarm of media covering the October 2001 Asia-Pacific Economic Cooperation summit in China's sparkling "super city"—more than 3,000 domestic and foreign reporters and 517 news organizations—would be sure to lap it up. The concept was brilliant and a public relations bull's-eye. The leaders of two countries, longtime antagonists, would sit down and talk at an appropriately named hotel. I had initially doffed my hat to the survey team that had come up with the idea the week before.

But symbolism and paper ideas often clash with reality. I dealt in reality. On further investigation by security sweepers, the luxurious ten-story Fairmont Peace Hotel, a five-star art deco marvel built in 1929, was, in the euphemistic argot of the National Security Council, "heavily affected."

In the more direct language of the WHCA agent who informed me of the problem, the conference room at the Peace Hotel that had been selected for the meeting between Bush and Putin was a "sieve"—though he modified "sieve" with a common expletive for greater effect.

I got the point. The room was so loaded with taps and listening devices that Bush and Putin might just as well have broadcast their secret talks to the world.

Meeting at the Peace Hotel was not a good idea. The last-minute news after the sweep arrived at midnight the day before the talks were to take place.

It was not my idea, but I had to take responsibility. I had to find a solution.

George W. Bush, still reeling from the horrific September 11 attacks in New York, Washington, and Pennsylvania only weeks before, was still formulating his plans for his "War on Terror."

The world was watching, on edge. After the attacks, Bush immediately canceled a September trip to China, Japan, and South Korea. In mid-September Chinese Foreign Minister Tang Jiaxuan met in Washington with Vice President Dick Cheney and Secretary of State Colin Powell to affirm China's strong support for the American global anti-terrorism efforts and arranged for Bush to come to Shanghai to meet those country's leaders at the APEC (Asia-Pacific Economic Cooperation) summit over three days, beginning on October 18.

From a strict advance perspective, the trip was fraught with land mines.

Adding the meeting with Vladimir Putin created the potential for total disaster. There were far too many variables and too little time. To make things even more interesting, in July that year Russia and China had agreed to a twenty-year treaty that called for economic and military cooperation between the two countries.

The talks between Bush and Putin in Shanghai would be frank and center on Russian contributions to the US initiative to rid

Afghanistan of the Taliban and discuss sharing intelligence that would benefit the nascent US effort there. The two would also discuss missile defense and nuclear-force cuts.

The talks between Bush and Putin would be crucial and sensitive. The Chinese were not invited to attend. There was no doubt they would have loved to have had a place at the table to hear what the Americans and Russians were up to.

The stated theme of the summit, attended by leaders from its twenty-one Pacific Rim members, including Australia, Brunei, China, Chile, the Republic of Korea, Malaysia, Mexico, the Philippines, New Zealand, Singapore, Thailand, and Japan, was "Meeting New Challenges in the New Century."

In Washington, caught in the whirlwind, I knew I would have a few challenges of my own.

Shanghai was barely controlled chaos, with more than sixty planes carrying leaders to the summit. And if the political leaders and their entourages were not enough, General Motors CEO John Smith Jr., AOL Time-Warner CEO Gerald Levin, Hewlett-Packard CEO and future presidential candidate Carly Fiorina, and Microsoft founder Bill Gates would also attend.

Our survey team had preceded the onslaught to Shanghai and had come back with a plan. Holding Bush and Putin's ultrasecret discussions at the Peace Hotel seemed a masterstroke of political theater, sure to take center stage.

In Shanghai, I checked in to the Portman Hotel in Shanghai Center, part of a stunning complex that rose gracefully above West Nanjiing Road like a modern-day Emerald City of Oz.

In my room, thinking about the meeting the next day between Bush and Putin, I had a number of concerns. Still, I had to agree that holding the talks at the Peace Hotel was a public relations bonanza. The symbolism at such a difficult time in American history would be rich. The message would be clear and positive.

First glances can be myopic and are never good in advance work.

It was midnight when the director of the White House Communications Agency sweep team, the guys with the knowledge and the sensitive equipment to find anything, called me in my room at the Portman and announced the results of their thorough check of the conference room at the Peace Hotel. He informed me that the room where the talks between Bush and Putin were to take place was full of eavesdropping devices.

We'd have to find another venue.

I immediately called my boss, Brian Montgomery, and told him. I made a second call to Mary Haines, a highly respected National Security Council operative I felt was one of the best people to deal with in these all too common and often frantic last-minute assaults.

"We need to find another room."

It was not necessary for me to add "immediately."

Then I made a third call to my Russian counterpart, Alexander Marshalov, first deputy and head of presidential foreign policy, a man I had worked with in the past and got along with. In the background I heard laughter and the inevitable clinking of glasses I knew were filled with vodka. Marshalov was a master of protocol, a survivor of the demanding and unforgiving Russian bureaucracy that, above all else, required participants to do their jobs and never rock the boat. Russians in the system who rose through the ranks like Marshalov were survivors.

"You have to be kidding me," Marshalov told me. "That's impossible. We will do it at the Peace Hotel."

"No," I said.

Marshalov hung up.

I knew his next call would be to the Kremlin. It was getting late, and I was tired. I knew also that the Russians would be just as loath as the Americans to hold talks in a sieve, regardless of whomever had planted the bugs. At that hour it didn't matter. Both our heads were on the guillotine. He had not survived the Russian system by being impulsive.

I waited. I knew a team of Russians would be screening the conference room at the Peace Hotel.

An hour later he called back.

"We checked, and you're right."

As I waited for Marshalov's call, I began making arrangements to move the talks to the Portman, where the American delegation was staying. It would be a frantic effort, but I knew we'd be two steps ahead of the Chinese. They'd have no time to install any devices or taps at the Portman.

We cleared a room, secured it, and informed the Russians of the change of venue. They agreed.

George Bush and Vladimir Putin held their talks.

At a press conference later, Putin would tell the assembled media that "in our assessment, in the Russian assessment, the meeting was really productive and useful. It was a forthright and trustful talk."

When it was his turn, George Bush would say that "after the events of the last five weeks, we can report positive progress."

Only the participants knew what was actually discussed during the meeting at the Portman, but I was happy to know that the Chinese were not among the listeners.

I was also relieved that things had worked out, last-minute alarms aside.

To vent my accumulated agita, I joined the Portman's general manager, a genuine character and certifiable eccentric, for a ride around Shanghai, sitting in the sidecar of his Harley-Davidson, working our way through the busy streets of the Jing'an District in the energetic city center, waving and greeting passersby.

It was a perfect end to another hectic trip.

I can admit now, years later, that cocktails were involved.

CHAPTER 23

Shining Path

PERU'S SHINING PATH GUERRILLAS WERE A PARTICULARLY ODIOUS group whose violence raised the eyebrows of even the most ardent leftist revolutionaries. To the Shining Path, murdering innocent people was neither brutal nor uncalled for.

To its leader, Abimael Guzman, a professor of philosophy, violence was merely useful symbolism in his quest to champion the rights of the peasant farmers and indigenous people of Peru.

Guzman was not a proponent of pursuing his cause through academic debate or political discourse, and he'd been refining his unique form of vicious protest since the late 1970s. Tens of thousands of Peruvians paid for his efforts with their lives.

In 1980, the day after Christmas, while the rest of the country celebrated Peru's first elections after seventeen years of military dictatorship, Shining Path guerrillas celebrated Mao Tse Tung's birthday by killing mongrel dogs and hanging them from streetlamps in the center of Lima.

Apparently, Guzman had a thing for dogs. He frequently compared community leaders and politicians to them. As a devout Maoist, a fading ideology among the day's revolutionaries, Guzman had an affection for the Chinese leader's birthday as well. In late December 1992, the Shining Path let loose some twenty dogs strapped with dynamite in central Lima, then blew them up.

A study by Peru's Truth and Reconciliation Commission, established in 2001 to study the country's violent past, found that some seventy thousand Peruvians were killed or had disappeared between 1980 and 2000. Half those deaths were attributed to the actions of the Shining Path; more than a third, to the Peruvian military and police.

When George W. Bush announced he would make a two-day visit to Lima for a bilateral summit meeting with President Alejandro Toledo on March 23, 2002, I knew the planning and the visit itself would not be a walk in the park. I hoped to arrange a summit that would avoid any contact with the Shining Path, but I knew also that I would be dealing with the Peruvian military and police.

George Bush was an avid proponent and voice of America's anti-communist policy wherever he went, and the Shining Path had long made its hatred for what it considered "American imperialism" known. The Peruvian police had a reputation for doings things their own way, on their own schedule.

My job in Lima was an unsettling prospect.

When the regional security officer at the American embassy in Peru told me things were under cautious control, I was not exactly relieved. I knew an American president in the Shining Path's backyard was simply too much of a temptation for the dog-obsessed Guzman.

George Bush would be the first sitting American president to visit the country, part of an initiative to strengthen ties with Latin America that included stops in Bolivia, Colombia, and Ecuador.

It was a whirlwind tour, and my charge was to make sure the trip to Peru ran smoothly and without incident.

As was my practice, I headed to Lima with my team of ten from Washington a week before. My first stop was the American embassy, a large modern and imposing building in the residential area of Monterrico, on Avenida La Encalada.

I shook my head when I saw it. I had always wondered why Americans built such large, attention-attracting buildings for their embassies. Pride certainly; but these edifices often proved to be magnets for abuse—and the first place that mobs or more sinister players would attack when American policy aroused long-simmering anger, which was frequently.

Why not just erect a flashing neon light: "Attack here"?

I thought about Teheran and the hostage crisis in 1979, and the destruction of the American embassy in Islamabad the same year. Add the 1983 car bombing at the embassy in Beirut that killed thirty-two Lebanese, seventeen Americans, and fourteen visitors, and the simultaneous attacks on the embassies in Nairobi and Dar es Salaam in 1998, and the pattern was inescapable. Grand and inviting embassies, often with poor protection, made no sense to me.

The Shining Path were no strangers to car bombs and had already set one off outside the embassy in Lima in 1993.

I met the embassy's Marine security guard in the foyer, and he led me to the office of the embassy's regional security officer, the man who kept his ear to the ground in Peru. I knew he could fill me in on the latest news about the illusive Shining Path as well as anyone.

"There have been some recent threats," he told me, "but with the Shining Path, threats are always there. We have nothing specific. Act with caution."

Small comfort, but it was all I had to go on.

We had been discreet about our arrival, as we always were. Low profiles in the advance business were pro forma. But I knew operatives from the Shining Path were aware we had arrived. A large presence of Americans in Lima organizing an American president's visit would not go unnoticed.

I only hoped that we were not important enough to blow up.

I would be wrong.

Two days before George Bush would arrive in Lima to meet with President Toledo, the advance team had finished a busy day, coordinating schedules, checking with local police on their security efforts, and securing the summit room, the post-meeting press conference, and organizing George Bush's final motorcade departure to Jorge Chavez International Airport, six miles outside the city.

Ten of us gathered for dinner downtown at a pleasant outdoor café, checking notes and relaxing as best any of us could in the middle of organizing a bilateral meeting in the home of the Shining Path.

We had barely dug into our entrees when a car screeched to the curb in front of us.

Out jumped several embassy security people.

"Get back to your hotel immediately," one yelled anxiously. "There has been an explosion. We will escort you. When you get there, go immediately to your rooms and stay there."

The bombing had occurred at a mall four blocks from the embassy, outside a seven-story hotel and a branch of the Banco de Crédito del Peru. Nine people were killed and thirty injured.

I did not have to guess the perpetrators.

In my room at the Lima Marriott, I took a deep breath and called Joe Hagen, White House deputy chief of staff for operations.

"We are all fine," I told him, "but the shit has hit the fan here. Call off the trip?"

Hagen assured me that George Bush would not be deterred and the visit was on.

"Two-bit terrorists aren't going to prevent me from doing what we need to do, and that is to promote our friendship in the hemisphere. Our neighborhood is important to us. Peru is an important country. You bet I'm going," George Bush told reporters at a press conference in Washington before he left.

I hung up and immediately took a second call, this one from the embassy's regional security officer.

He did not mince his words. It was early in the investigation, he told me, but all indications were that whoever had planted the bomb had the wrong hotel. The explosion and chaos hours before had been meant for the White House advance team.

I took a deep breath, and it was not from lack of oxygen in the high-altitude Lima air.

Still at the Marriott the next morning, unsure at that point of the status of the trip, several of my staff asked for more information on the attack the night before. I decided it would not be expedient to mention that intelligence indicated it had been intended for us.

We met in the Marriott's restaurant for breakfast and a discussion of the day's duties as Panamericana Television broadcast scenes taped at the site of the explosion. The national network clearly had no content restrictions.

The broadcast was gruesome, with severed legs isolated on the street as well as a headless torso. In a country where the Shining Path had wreaked havoc for years, horror was routine daytime news.

George Bush would arrive the next day. We still had much work to do.

As we sat in the Marriott watching the broadcast, redundantly, I felt, Peruvian Interior Minister Fernando Rospigliosi told the press, "There's no doubt the explosion is connected to the events of September 11 and the presence of President Bush."

The game was on.

In Lima, I was coordinating security efforts with lead Secret Service agent John Bush, no relation to the president, with whom I had a great working relationship in the past.

We met outside the hotel to be free of any possible passersby listening.

Peru had long been a neglected stepchild in American foreign relations, with little strategic or economic value to our global plans. The Peruvians and Alejandro Toledo in particular were excited for a chance to stand on the world stage. But they were unused to the clamor and logistics involved in a summit meeting with the president of the United States and the large group of aides and advisors who would accompany him.

Throw in the bombing from the night before and the lingering threat of what the Shining Path had waiting, and I found myself in a full-blown nightmare while I was wide awake.

"As far as the bilateral," John Bush told me, "no surprises. It's basically disorganized."

I stared at him in the morning sunlight outside our hotel.

He was not finished with his assessment.

"We're getting all kinds of information that points to chaos."

I was inured to chaos. I had grown almost comfortable with last-minute snafus, logistical snares, and the inevitable clash of egos that accompany any presidential trip, but Lima was beginning to look like a new frontier.

After I said goodbye to John Bush, I did what I always did. I called a meeting of my people and apprised them of the situation. Then we went over our plans again, in painstaking detail. I knew I could do nothing about the Shining Path, but I was determined that the short summit meeting would go off precisely as we had laid it out—as the expression goes, if it was the last thing I'd do.

And with the Shining Path lurking in the background, I thought to myself in a bit of dark humor, it just *might* be the last thing I'd do.

I can attest that the old saying "practice makes perfect," trite and tired as it is, holds water.

The short summit went well. Alejandro Toledo proved to be amiable and grateful, and George Bush was masterful in his knowledge of Peru and the value of collegial relations between the two countries. Logistically, the short visit was flawless.

At a press conference after the summit, Toledo spoke to a gathering of reporters as George Bush stood by his side under the tightest security I had seen in my many years of advance work.

"This is a historic visit made by a friend representing a country with which we have had a historical relationship. It is not merely a diplomatic visit, it is an official working visit, and we have touched on substantive issues, which range from the open struggle against poverty, a war without quarter against terrorism and drug trafficking. I repeat, a war with no ambiguities whatsoever against terrorism and drug trafficking.

"We've touched on issues of trade, education, even the Peace Corps. But, my friend, George Bush, this Peru is a country that welcomes you with open arms. We are renewing our friendship, and this is the beginning of a new era in the relationship between us."

Bush was equally effusive.

"Peru is on the path toward greater freedom and greater prosperity, and America will be the partner in this progress.

"This relationship is based on common values and common interests. Our nations understand that political and economic progress depends on security—and that security is impossible in a world with terrorists. Peruvians have been reminded again this week of the terrible human toll of terror. On behalf of the people of the United States, I express our deep sympathy for the victims of the recent bombing and their loved ones."

Standing off to the side, I thought we had dodged a bullet, perhaps literally.

We had only to get George and Laura Bush to the airport in the morning and had planned the route meticulously. As is my wont, I had memorized it and knew the roads we would follow and what turns we'd make. Studying the maps beforehand, the trip to the airport would be simple.

I imagined I saw a slim, glimmering shaft of light for the first time on the trip. That, of course, called to mind another old saw: That light you see at the end of the tunnel could be a train coming in your direction.

Threats from the Shining Path notwithstanding, enthusiastic crowds lined the route four and five screaming and cheering people deep. There were no barriers or extra security forces to hold them back.

In the lead car with John Bush, following a police escort, with the president and Laura Bush in the limousine behind us, we could barely move as we inched through the throngs. Apparently, the Peruvian police were not overly concerned.

Two blocks in, the police escort turned left when I knew it should have gone right. In an instant, the entire motorcade was surrounded by cheering and excited Peruvians.

I turned to the presidential limousine behind us and saw a very animated George W. Bush. He did not look happy.

John Bush immediately jumped from our car and ran back to the presidential limousine and joined seven other Secret Service agents who had done the same, surrounding it as it made a half-hearted attempt to gain speed.

I jumped on the radio to try to coordinate the escape.

Things were growing very tense, and it was clear the local police had no interest in helping. They were enjoying the sight of the American president caught in the throng of their adoring countrymen.

On the radio with the agent in charge of the president's limousine, I heard only obscenities.

The mob quickly parted as the aggressive agent driving the limousine made it clear he was not stopping.

It took close to forty-five very fraught minutes to reach the airport. I had planned for fifteen.

We made it to the airport without a serious incident—and, more important, without stopping.

My heart was pounding as we reached the tarmac in front of Air Force One.

George Bush stepped out and looked directly at me. He raised his hands, palms up, and shrugged his shoulders as he stared at me.

I did not need a body language expert to understand what he was telling me. The polite version would be: "What the hell was that all about?"

CHAPTER 24

The Showdown at Putin's Dacha

It would be an understatement to say I was alarmed in May 2002 as I watched the armed Russian guards at Vladimir Putin's dacha outside Moscow close the massive iron gates behind President George W. Bush's limousine as we stood outside, our mouths agape.

For me, that afternoon and everything attached to it moved in excruciatingly slow motion. As I stood outside the gates, visions of the worst possible outcome seemed quite real.

George Bush was inside without his usual Secret Service detail, with no access to his normal state-of-the-art communications systems, including the proverbial "football."

The heavy iron gates were closed, and we stood outside, helpless.

Vladimir Putin played well with others when it suited his purposes. That afternoon he had chosen not to, and we were lucky he wanted only to make a statement and not start a war.

At the time, Putin's burgeoning post-9/11 friendship with George W. Bush was in full bloom. The two had met at Bush's ranch in rural Crawford, Texas, only months before. I stood outside Putin's dacha frozen in fear, quickly checking off possible solutions, trying to control my panic, and searching for an answer about what had just happened.

I felt as if I had just been sucker-punched, and in a way, I had. The scene, as they say in the advance business, was a nightmare.

In 2023, for good reason, Vladimir Putin is an international pariah with few allies. The animosity between President Joe Biden and Putin is palpable, their contempt for each other plain. Putin's invasion of Ukraine has made that certain.

Things were starkly different in 2002, when George W. Bush and Putin appeared to have signed a mutual admiration treaty.

It was a puzzling partnership from my perspective, because I knew of Putin's darker side and did not trust him. I was wary of him, suspicious of his motives, of his machismo and his subterfuge. He had not risen through the ranks of the KGB and flourished in the cutthroat world of Russian politics through kindness and respect for his peers.

Thinking about the incident at Putin's dacha now, I am chilled at how close we came to losing control over the safety and well-being of George W. Bush.

At the time, the two were in the early stages of a blossoming "bromance," a rare flirtation between the leaders of two countries that had been at each other's throats for years. The months after 9/11 and George Bush's nascent war on terror had made for strange bedfellows, none stranger than Bush and Putin.

The world was amazed. I was not.

Even in 2002 I knew Vladimir Putin was the sort of leader who'd welcome you at the front door, smile, and politely invite you inside. I also knew he was the sort of leader who held a knife behind his back as he did so, waiting for the first chance to eviscerate you.

The president's safety while he was in Moscow was my responsibility, and I remained cautious. It is clear to me now that I was not cautious enough.

George W. Bush and Vladimir Putin's relationship was a knotted entanglement of feints and shadows, with each man sparring for the best possible outcome. My advance team and the American Secret Service, despite our best due diligence, became unwitting victims of a Putin masterstroke that afternoon.

We all had inadvertently given Putin an opportunity to settle a perceived slight no one on the American side was aware of.

The showdown at the dacha, thankfully, from my perspective, did not get a lot of press coverage because the press was not privy to the tensions at the front gate.

We felt we were prepared for George W. Bush's trip to Moscow. The choreography we'd painstakingly created in Washington months before the meeting with Putin in Moscow proved useless.

With stopwatch precision, we had laid out meeting times for the bilateral summit between Bush and Putin in Moscow and St. Petersburg to the minute. We had listed each Russian and American participant, with phone and email information for everyone involved in three days of talks between President George W. Bush and Putin on what everyone hoped would become a new nuclear weapons accord that would slash warheads by more than two-thirds over ten years—the Strategic Offensive Reductions Treaty.

We had meticulously imagined every possible scenario and devised plans to accommodate each. We had stipulated precise travel routes around Moscow and St. Petersburg, including who would travel in which vehicle. We had even diagrammed where participants would sit at various conference and dining tables.

We did not know that all our painstaking planning had gone off the rails months before in Texas. Putin felt disrespected and planned his payback.

Unaware of the Texas problem, my biggest concern for the Moscow summit, one that had made me uncomfortable from the moment I heard about it, was that George and Laura Bush would stay overnight at Putin's dacha near Moscow. It seemed to me incautious and overly trusting, a sign that the so-called bromance between the two leaders had gone too far.

George Bush might have trusted Vladimir Putin, but I didn't. Having Bush spend the night in enemy territory might have appeared to be a bright and shining moment of détente, but to me, frankly, it was stupid and unnecessary—gilding the lily for no practical purpose.

Bush in the dacha meant for us a certain loss of control, a dangerous precedent that put our usually watertight communications systems in jeopardy. No matter what we did, no matter how many sweeps we made beforehand, our vital communications would likely be compromised.

The lack of control made me nervous.

It was not my job to question such decisions. My job was to make certain we did everything we could to keep things under our control. To that end, the advance team and I rehearsed every possible scenario of the two-day visit. As usual I drilled everyone on their responsibilities to the point of irritation.

On the way to Moscow before the meetings, I felt certain we'd covered everything. At the time, I did not know about a set-to in Crawford between our Secret Service team and Putin's security people.

To make certain my Russian counterparts were on board with our plans, I flew to Moscow five days before the summit and met with them around a large oak table in the Kremlin, the echoes of its dark history muted but evident. These were men I'd get to know intimately over the next four years as Putin and George W. Bush continued to meet on the world stage.

There was Igor Shuvalov, Putin's chief of staff, and Dmitri Peskov, Putin's press secretary, who, twenty-one years later, was still handling Putin's contentious and self-serving announcements on why his decimation of Ukraine was for the good of the Russian Union.

To make sure I did not miss any of the nuance of the intentionally opaque language of diplomacy, I brought with me the American embassy's counselor for political affairs, George Krol, a Harvard and Oxford graduate and an experienced Sovietologist who proved invaluable in directing discussions about our concerns.

I think that without George Krol's calm assistance, my anxiety over the Bushes' stay at Putin's dacha would have been off the wall.

As I left the Kremlin, I felt vaguely assured we had covered all the necessary bases. Vague assurances, though, are not conducive to a good night's sleep, and I spend most of my week at the Moscow Marriott staring at the ceiling.

The great irony of that horrible afternoon outside the locked gates of Putin's dacha was that neither our meticulous planning nor my lengthy meetings with George Krol and the Russians at the Kremlin had anything to do with what happened that afternoon.

The Bushes' abduction—and it was an abduction—was the price we paid for a turf war at George Bush's Crawford ranch months before, in November 2001. No one from the Secret Service had alerted me that Putin's security people were upset about being cut off from Putin on the ranch by the Americans.

If the Bush and Putin relationship had blossomed into a bromance by Moscow, the meeting in Crawford was like a successful first date.

Putin and Bush would visit Crawford High School, where Bush would tell a packed gymnasium of cheering students, "We had a great dinner last night. We had a little Texas barbecue, pecan pie, a little Texas music. And I think the president really enjoyed himself."

Putin, standing beside Bush, grinned widely.

Putin was not apparently grinning widely later that day when he heard his security detail had been cut off from their duties on the ranch by the Secret Service. A minor dustup, I would hear much later, long after the incident in Moscow; nothing of any consequence, the Secret Service would assure me.

The Russians felt disrespected. Putin took note. The Russians had been offended, and if I know the Russians, they began planning their payback immediately.

It was as simple as that. The hugely embarrassing and potentially serious incident at the front gate of Putin's dacha was nothing more than the Russians settling a score. It had nothing to do with diplomacy or sensitive negotiations or rapprochement.

It had everything to do with saving face. That was how it worked with the Russians. They were polite and seemingly accommodating, but I was never sure of their motives.

Putin was sensitive to perceived insults. Putin noticed everything.

As I stood outside the dacha's gates, the Americans were about to get served a nice big helping of humble pie.

It happened in a panicked blur. George W. Bush was inside the compound at Putin's dacha near Moscow surrounded by Russian security. With him in "the Beast," his presidential limousine, were his wife, Laura, and two Secret Service agents. Ironically, given the reason for Bush's meeting with Putin, Bush was without the "football"—the nondescript black leather briefcase containing the top-secret nuclear war plan and launch codes.

The instant the Beast passed into Putin's compound, Russian security closed the main gate and moved in front of it.

The football, the man assigned to carry it, and the rest of the always robust security detail we brought along for any trip was with me and a group of stunned other Americans, locked outside the gates, staring anxiously into the compound.

It was an unprecedented and frightening event. Such a thing had simply never happened before on any presidential trip. Bush's essential protection had been severed so quickly we could only stare, aghast at the possibilities. The Secret Service had been duped. We had all been duped.

Outside the locked gates with me was an SUV holding Secretary of State Colin Powell; Bush's chief of staff, Andrew Card; and Secretary of Commerce Donald Evans.

It was, as they say in the advance business, a worst-case scenario.

I was not happy.

Neither was Andy Card. I walked briskly to the passenger side of Card's Ford Tahoe as he lowered the window.

"What the hell is going on?" he asked.

"I'm not sure," I told him.

"Maybe you should call Condoleezza Rice and get some answers," I suggested gingerly.

Though I oversaw the timing and logistics of the entire trip, it was not my job to order the president's chief of staff to do anything. But the enormity of what was happening pushed me close to doing that.

Rice, the National Security Advisor, was at the Moscow Marriott. She would know how to get to the bottom of the confusion. She had access to the Russians responsible for the chaos, not that they would likely be forthcoming. Whatever was going on was neither an accident nor an oversight on the Russians' part.

My job was to assure that these sorts of harrowing incidents did not happen.

Whatever statement the inscrutable Putin had planned to make with his blockade at the front gate had potentially ominous results. As much as we tried, as suspicious as we were about his motives, we could not read him.

This was precisely the type of incident I was charged with preventing.

My mouth was as dry as a desert floor. I had my own channels.

I immediately called Igor Shuvalov, Putin's chief of staff, who was in his office at the Kremlin. I had been dealing with him for weeks to iron out the torrent of small details that accompany such a meeting between two heads of state.

"I can do nothing about this," he told me calmly.

"What do you mean?" I asked, incredulous.

"It is a security issue," he said.

At that moment, my job was on the line.

We were staring at a huge national security crisis and international embarrassment.

"Igor, do something," I pleaded.

Andy Card called Condoleezza Rice, still at the hotel.

It was clear that the situation would have to be resolved by officials higher up the command ladder than Shuvalov and me. We would have to wait.

I suspect it was simply a matter of Putin waiting long enough to make his point: Don't disrespect my security forces.

He made his point emphatically with me. After that tsunami, I made certain to do a thorough background check on any past meetings, making sure we had not stepped on any toes.

As I waited outside the still-locked gates, I could see below me George Bush and Vladimir Putin strolling through the estate's gardens, seemingly without a care in the world.

Bush had to have sensed the chaos outside the gate as we all stared impotently from outside. If he was upset or nervous or concerned about his safety, he gave no sign. He appeared to be enjoying himself.

The worrying was my job.

I knew as things began to gel and the front gates opened to let the American delegation in that I still had a job.

Putin had made his point.

I had learned a painful but valuable lesson.

The next morning, as I returned to the dacha for their luggage (I was the only one allowed inside), I found Condoleezza Rice playing a soothing Rachmaninoff piano concerto as George Bush sat to the side, cigar in hand.

It seemed to me an incongruous moment after the chaos of the day before.

All was well.

CHAPTER 25

Évian

THE TRANQUIL, STUNNINGLY BEAUTIFUL FRENCH VILLAGE OF ÉVI-an-les-Bains, France, has drawn the elite to its spas, grand hotels, and eponymous mineral water for two centuries. Sitting bucolically on the shores of Lake Geneva, Évian has long attracted royals and celebrities seeking respite and healing from the tensions and pressures of their elevated workaday world.

By the time I left Évian in June 2003, after running interference for the myriad problems of the twenty-ninth G8 Summit, I should have gone back for a month to restore my bruised mental health and well-being.

But I was neither a royal nor a celebrity. I shook it off and returned to Washington, still collecting my wits. By then my skin had grown thick, but the trip was a nonstop, breath-holding sprint to keep ahead of catastrophe.

There were anti-globalization protests in Geneva, our first stop on the way to the summit. There were icy relations between George W. Bush—campaigning to attract allies for his new war in Iraq—and French President Jacques Chirac and German Chancellor Gerhard Schröder, who were lukewarm about the prospect. There was a special one-off and highly secret meeting with Chinese President Hu Jintao, who was in Évian, though not part of the summit.

There was my legitimately appalled French counterpart, the urbane French ambassador for the summit, Monsieur LeBeouf, his mouth agape as our huge American helicopters stormed the quiet alpine town.

Armed with diagrams and charts outlining our arrival, I had met LeBoeuf to explain our plans for the summit. As was our wont, these did not follow his own carefully laid out schedule, which all the other participants had agreed to.

Sitting across from me at our first meeting with a look of resigned acceptance that he had no power to change our plans, he looked at me.

"Mr. Swift," he said with barely concealed frustration, "you are aware of the protocol."

"I am," I told him, adding perhaps unnecessarily to the experienced diplomat, "but I must change that protocol."

"This is impossible," he replied.

But he knew it was not impossible. He knew we would do things our way.

And we both knew neither of us could do a thing about it.

We were both experienced—two realistic government officials dealing with decisions that were not our own. Over seven very hectic days in Évian, we forged a close alliance built on our mutual understanding of the jobs we had to do and our places in the larger scheme of things.

That respect engendered a wry, tongue-in-cheek rapport that, even in the always tense round-peg-in-square-hole approach the Americans took at Évian, brought a smile to my face.

At one point, as the massive invasion force of American helicopters began to set down, LeBoeuf turned to me, his voice barely discernible above the roar of the rotor blasts.

"You know, Judd, this is not Vietnam."

I understood completely.

Key among the other problems at the summit was Évian itself. On one hand, what better place for world leaders to meet than a town known for its healing and serenity? On paper, Évian was symbolically perfect.

On the other hand, for me and my advance team, getting the massive American presence into the tiny town without incident was like threading a needle while standing on the deck of a rolling ship.

The clinical term we used for our summit plans, our "footprint," was precise, at least theoretically. In Évian, logistics and geography amplified our always size 15 EEE footprint beyond human understanding—at least that of LeBeouf, and no doubt observers from other attending countries, who knew better than to complain about the Americans publicly.

Americans did not go gently into summit meetings. The art of diplomacy requires tact and subtlety, with delicate, precise steps that announce strength, confidence, and respect for the opinions of others. I felt that Americans emphasized the strength part of the equation far too much. Showing our power was essential at international meetings while the world watched, and it was perhaps comforting to our allies, though definitely annoying. I could see it written large on the faces of my counterparts:

"Here come the Americans. Head for cover."

We came into every summit like a bull in a china shop, while all the other participants followed protocol. In the Alpine tightness of Évian, our arrival was close to cacophonic. I would understand if others viewed our entrances as a not-too-subtle form of bullying. Our forcefulness did little to show our respect for other countries.

That was how we did it, and I had no control over it. My job was to manage it as best I could.

With the war in Iraq then more than two months old, the theme for the gathering leaders in Évian, organized by French President Jacques Chirac, was "solidarity, responsibility, security, and democracy."

In those days, the annual summits began to take on the appearance of an Old Boys' Club. Leaders knew one another, knew the domestic problems facing their counterparts, and were genuinely interested in working out the international issues they faced with legitimate debate and discussion. Gerhard Schröder of Germany, Silvio Berlusconi of Italy, Junichiro Koizumi of Japan, Vladimir Putin of Russia, Tony Blair of the United Kingdom, and Jean Chrétien of Canada would join George W. Bush for face-to-face meetings to test their resolve over the growing tensions in the Middle East and also focus on growing problems in Africa, including HIV/AIDS.

There were underlying problems at Évian. The Old Boys' Club was fighting. When leaders are upset with one another, the demands on the support staff at a summit grow even tenser. If something goes wrong, some small and seemingly insignificant detail that upsets the flow, the support staff pays the price.

George W. Bush was already tense; he had just started a war that some of his colleagues at the summit were unhappy about. He had recently pushed through the US Congress a $15 billion program to fight AIDS and had chided his European counterparts for not doing more about AIDS and alleviating African poverty and world hunger.

That would all be on the table in Évian.

US State Department spokesman James Rubin was blunt about the upcoming discussions.

"The G8 Summit is about personal chemistry, and there are two big problems," Rubin said. "The president thinks Schröder lied to him, and the president thinks that Jacques Chirac screwed him."

Another European official described hope for the summit concisely:

"One hears people in the US administration saying that the Americans should punish the French, ignore the Germans, and make peace with the Russians.

"Well, that may be what people may feel and indeed think. But if that is the strategy that America pursues, then it will be very hard to get an agreement in Évian over how to move forward on the world economy."

I had too much on my plate to worry excessively, but those comments did not encourage a feeling of confidence in me.

Administration higher-ups were tense. Anxieties trickle down. If the right car is not in the right place when expected, I'd hear about it.

For the advance team, getting the large American presence at Évian was particularly challenging, and we spent countless hours drawing up plans and painstakingly preparing diagrams showing timing and the order of the American procession into town. The American delegation was enormous, with hundreds of press and presidential staff, including the Secret Service complement, cabinet members and their staffs, and the usual hangers-on.

George W. Bush brought with him to Évian his heavy hitters, Secretary of State Colin Powell and National Security Advisor Condoleezza Rice, an indication of the seriousness of the summit. Their presence always amped up the need for more security and more staff.

Flying to Geneva would be George W. Bush on Air Force One, followed by six other aircraft, including a second Boeing 747, and smaller planes, including a special communications plane bedecked in mysterious antennae. Meeting us in Geneva for the short trip to Évian would be seven large Sea Stallion helicopters to carry the president and his large posse the final twenty-five miles to Évian.

Awaiting us in Geneva were our friends from the anti-globalization movement, the same people we had dodged two years before in Genoa. They had not softened, nor were they waiting with open arms. Protesters, some wearing black hoods, rampaged through shops around Lake Geneva. Two suspended themselves with ropes from a bridge and unveiled a banner. Others disrupted traffic, and hundreds more rioted in downtown Geneva.

Police responded with tear gas, rubber bullets, and water hoses.

For me, it was an expected though distant welcome. We had planned to be in and out of Geneva quickly, and we were.

The problems began as we made our way to Évian. Ours was a mammoth undertaking that stood in stark contrast to the operations of the other countries attending. The United States simply does things on a large scale.

In addition to the torrent of details I was charged with arranging, I needed landing zones for the helicopters to ferry support staff and press across the lake, secure rooms for sensitive discussions, and buses and cars for everyone to get quickly to their assigned hotels, details of which my teams had already worked out. The Sea Stallion copters we brought in from an American base in Italy could lift tanks. Landing or taking off, they could easily tear off roofs.

Our French hosts had planned for the parties of each country to cross the lake into Évian by boat to better accommodate the village's narrow streets and lack of parking for the usual storm of limousines full of dignitaries and support vehicles full of luggage.

My team arranged for the throng of press and the large group of American civil servants and support staff to follow the plan to cross the lake by boat.

George W. Bush or, more likely, his staff decided to eschew the boat trip.

He would instead fly into Évian on Marine One, I was told.

The pressures of last-minute scheduling and coordinating immediately grew exponentially. I now had two arrivals to set up, which included dealing with transportation for luggage and accommodations and arrival times.

The president's arrival was the most important.

I had to find a landing spot that could accommodate the large helicopter, and I chose a small hill overlooking the village to accommodate the pressing security concerns. Americans, especially George W. Bush, were at the time extremely unpopular, and various terrorist organizations were growing stronger in the wake of 9/11. I had to also arrange for twenty-five vehicles to be standing by to take the presidential party into Évian.

The hill was isolated, easily controlled, and large enough to accommodate the six incoming helicopters bearing George W. Bush and his party, who would be the last to arrive on the code-named Nighthawk 1. The timing of these arrivals was tricky. Nighthawk 6 had to arrive, drop its passengers, and depart before Nighthawk 5 arrived next. There simply was not enough room, and I knew in the tight confines of the hilltop, the disruptions from the rotors would be irritating at best.

I underestimated their force. Nighthawk 5 quickly removed a row of loose tiles on the nearby chalet we had commandeered as a temporary headquarters. Nighthawk 4 blew down a small tree.

I arrived as quickly as possible, allowing me enough time to meet on the hill with lead Secret Service agent Joe Ellis to survey the scene. We had forty minutes until Marine One, bearing President Bush and his wife, Laura, would arrive.

Ellis and I had earlier set up a perimeter and had a squadron of Secret Service and armed Marines on hand for a show of force we knew would give terrorists pause. The situation was far from ideal, but I was confident.

As I was standing to the side of the landing zone with Ellis, surrounded by his agents and the Marines, two impeccably dressed women appeared, bearing bouquets of flowers. I had no idea who they were, and neither did Joe Ellis. How they were able to walk through our tight security remains a mystery. But there they were.

We invited them into the chalet and, through LeBoeuf, learned they were Évian dignitaries, there to welcome George W. Bush. LeBoeuf was utterly calm and seemed to take the surprise visitors in Gallic stride.

We had thirty minutes until Marine One was to arrive.

I called my supervisor, Brian Montgomery, still in the air aboard Nighthawk 3.

"We have a serious security breach here," I told him.

The was no time for equivocation, but looking at the two women, dressed to the nines and looking expectantly proud of their role in welcoming the president of the United States to Évian, I knew we were fine. It was a gut reaction, I admit now. But I was sure they were legitimate.

"We have to get rid of them," Montgomery told me.

I quickly saw a nightmare of bad press coverage: LOCAL OFFICIALS UNCEREMONIOUSLY BANNED FROM BUSH WELCOME.

Standing on that hill amid the chaos of whirling dust and flying debris kicked up by the helicopter rotors, I knew instinctively they were not a threat. It was risky, but my own instincts and LeBoeuf's calmness assured me.

"We need to let them in," I told Montgomery. Beside me, Joe Ellis concurred.

As surprised as we were at the unexpected intrusion of the two-woman Évian delegation, the biggest surprise was theirs.

Standing beside the landing zone when Marine One set down, I watched as their elegant skirts were thrown up over the heads, their bouquets nearly blown from their manicured hands, their neatly applied lipstick spreading across their cheeks from the force.

Stunned, they welcomed George W. Bush to Évian.

Crisis averted.

I had another waiting for me with far more global implications.

Jacques Chirac had invited Chinese President Hu Jintao to Évian for an informal meeting, and the Americans had jumped at the rare opportunity and scheduled a secret one-on-one meeting between Hu and George W. Bush.

I thought of the meeting in October 2022, when Hu, no longer president but still active in Chinese politics, was escorted, quite publicly and unceremoniously, from the annual party meeting in Beijing. The man had stayed around the circles of power, apparently, for another nearly twenty years, but clearly his power had faded. Chinese politics remained as impenetrable in 2022 as they had been in Évian in 2003.

The opportunity for the leaders of two of the world's greatest powers to speak face-to-face, out of the glare of the world's spotlight, was rare. The advance team, the communications people, and the Secret Service had to make certain it was flawless—and, most important, private.

LeBoeuf and his French team had set up a separate meeting room for George W. Bush and Hu to discuss, among other things, maintaining stability in a world at war, global economic growth, and how to fight the growing problem of terrorism. Two other items on the agenda would sound familiar today: controlling global epidemics and America's China policy with respect to Taiwan.

The meeting had been kept under wraps, but such things are impossible to keep secret. Many of the world's intelligence services would have loved to have a seat at the table. As was our custom, the White House communications crew did a thorough check of the room.

I was not surprised to learn that the room was heavily bugged.

I went immediately to Mary Haines, my favorite National Security Council contact, who was in Évian. I knew her as a woman whose judgment and poise under pressure were unparalleled. We had had this conversation before.

"The room is totally compromised," I told her. "We need another venue."

She understood the gravity of the situation and the need to act quickly.

We would move the meeting.

My friend LeBoeuf was not so understanding and took the announcement as an insult to France, but once again he understood that we were moving the meeting.

My next call was to my Chinese interlocutor, a tall and distinguished diplomat who was the number-two man at the Chinese embassy in Paris and who spoke impeccable English. My concerns over security were such that I asked him to meet me in the gardens outside my hotel. As we strolled through the garden, I told him we were moving the meeting—and I told him why.

"This can't be," he said.

"I'm sorry to report that it is," I replied. To ease the shock of the sudden announcement, I carefully explained precisely what we were doing and how the new arrangements would look.

The odd thing about my garden conversation was that while the Chinese diplomat on the ground in Évian did not know about the sudden change in venue, his supervisors in Beijing already did.

Such was modern communications.

While I was announcing the sudden move, Mary Haines and her crew set up another meeting room in the president's suite in the hotel.

The meeting between George W. Bush and Hu went off on schedule and flawlessly. Only a few of us were aware of how close it had come to being canceled.

It was just another day in the world of advance.

I met with my new friend LeBoeuf as the dust settled, literally. I had grown to like him and his stoic manner in dealing with our loudness and bluster.

As we shook hands, both grateful as the summit closed that we had averted a series of what could have been major incidents, I thought to myself how easily we had worked together because we understood each other and, most important, trusted each other.

If only the diplomats and leaders had the same mutual respect and honesty in dealing with one another, the world's problems would be far more easily handled, I thought.

Index